RISING BEYOND BULLYING TRAUMA

OTHER TITLES BY RIA BERKHOUT

Breaking the Sugar Habit (ebook and audio book)

Don't be a Puppet (ebook and audio book)

The Art of Relationship Building (ebook and audio book)

RISING BEYOND BULLYING TRAUMA

A TEEN'S JOURNEY
from **PAIN** to **POWER**,
CONFIDENCE, and **JOY**

RIA BERKHOUT

Published 2025 by Gildan Media LLC
aka G&D Media
www.GandDmedia.com

RISING BEYOND BULLYING TRAUMA. Copyright © 2025 by Ria Berkhout. All rights reserved.

No part of this book may be used, reproduced or transmitted in any manner whatsoever, by any means (electronic, photocopying, recording, or otherwise), without the prior written permission of the author, except in the case of brief quotations embodied in critical articles and reviews. No liability is assumed with respect to the use of the information contained within. Although every precaution has been taken, the author and publisher assume no liability for errors or omissions. Neither is any liability assumed for damages resulting from the use of the information contained herein.

For all inquiries, permission requests, or other requests regarding copyright or the use of the content of this book, please contact: Ria Berkhout: berkhoutria@gmail.com

Cover design by Tom McKeveny

Interior design by Meghan Day Healey of Story Horse, LLC

Library of Congress Cataloging-in-Publication Data is available upon request

ISBN: 978-1-7225-0728-2

10   9   8   7   6   5   4   3   2   1

*For my two beautiful daughters,
Joyce-Youandi and Liliane-Jasmin.
You have taught me more than
I could ever teach you.*

Contents

Foreword by Brian Proctor 9
Disclaimer 11
Preface 13

1 Hopeless.. 15

2 The Departure.. 19

3 Car Trouble 21

4 A Strange Encounter 23

5 Hope.. 31

6 Reunion 33

7 Thoughts and Habits: What Do You Say to Yourself?.... 41

8 Accepting Yourself... 49

9 Nutrition: What Do You Put in Your Mouth?............ 57

10 Lunch.. 67

11 Anger 75

12 Collapse 77

13 Putting It into Practice 81

14 Apologies.. 87

15 Why Bullying Occurs...................................... 91

16 Visualization and Connecting with Your Desires 95

17 Big News 107

18 Mirror Exercise... 111

19 What Energy Do You Emit?............................. 115

20 What Story Do You Tell Yourself? 121

21 You Are the Thinker..................................... 131

22 Vision Board.. 137

23 Morning Ritual... 155

24 Forgiveness 161

25 Surprise 167

26 Concert.. 171

    Appendix: A Discussion of Bullying 177

    Acknowledgments 193

    Resources 195

    About the Author 198

Foreword

I had the pleasure of meeting Ria Berkhout at an event in Belfast, Northern Ireland. I instantly resonated with her quiet and thoughtful strength. We had dinner one evening and met several times over the next few days. I learned that Ria had a deep desire to share her understanding in an area that is often misunderstood, and her desire was palpable. I could feel her emotional connection to share with the world what she knew could help millions of children and their families.

When Ria shared her manuscript with me for this book, which you are now holding in your hands, I instantly knew that it needed to reach a wider audience. Especially our young people, and their families and educators who care for them.

What struck me right away was the instant draw I felt to the chance encounter between the two main characters and how their friendship developed from that circumstance. It deeply touched my heart, and I had to keep reading to find out how the story ended. This is one of those rare books that really draws you in through storytelling, but leaves you changed through its message. It is easy to connect to the experiences either first-hand, because you have lived them or you know someone who has.

The way Ria wrote about the subject of bullying in our current society and its true impact on us all creates a deeper awareness and understanding of ourselves and our community. We observe this type of behavior everywhere, from our schools to the workplace and in politics. We have become numb to the noise and hardly notice the harm it is doing.

Not anymore!

This book will change all of that for you. The following pages will not only help you understand but also give you tools and resources to effectively address, manage, and ultimately resolve the hurt and pain. As a bonus in the way the pages unfold, we are guided on a journey of increasing our own self-image. The way we behave, act, and see ourselves in this world. The lessons Ria shares are timeless, and we all benefit from them.

I am grateful that she was willing to share her manuscript with me that day. It has changed the way I view bullying and has given me real, practical tools I now use to help others.

This book is in your hands for a reason. I know that it will touch you the way it touched me. This is not a story of sadness, it is a story of hope, of change, and of courage. Get ready for a shift in perspective. Enjoy!

—Brian Proctor
Author of *12 Easy Steps to Change Your Life*

Disclaimer

The author has made every effort to present accurate and up-to-date information in this book but cannot guarantee that the information is correct or suitable for your specific situation.

The results of relying on the information provided in this book may vary, and we make no guarantees regarding the outcome. While we genuinely believe that this information will assist you in achieving your goals, your results will be influenced by your willingness to take action as well as external factors beyond our control. By reading this book, you acknowledge the potential risks associated with pursuing your goals and accept full responsibility for your own results. You agree not to hold Ria Berkhout or her company responsible or make any claims or actions arising from your use of the information provided.

This book is based on the author's personal experiences and extensive interviews with psychologists, victims, bullies, teachers, and parents. Any resemblance to actual persons, living or deceased, or real events is purely coincidental.

Preface

Dear reader,

With great excitement and dedication, I present to you this book, which stems from my personal experience and in-depth research as well as close interaction with psychologists, bullies, victims, and parents of bullied children. This book is the result of an intense quest for insight and understanding into bullying and its impact on the lives of teenagers.

Within these pages, you will find a story that unfolds in the form of a novel. Set in France, it is the story of Max, a young teenager confronted with the painful reality of bullying at school. Max's experiences mirror the challenges, fears, and desires of many bullied teenagers worldwide. It is my hope that this book will not only represent their voices but serve as a beacon of hope and guidance.

This book presents more than a mere story. It offers insights, advice, and strategies to help bullied teenagers find their own strength and create a life of joy, harmony, and self-confidence. Through Max's journey and our interactions with the characters, we discover the resilience of the human spirit and the potential for transformation even in the most challenging times.

I am honored to have shared the stories of psychologists, bullies, victims, and parents. Their expertise, perspectives, and emotional involvement have enriched and deepened this book. My gratitude goes out to them for sharing their experiences and insights, which serve as a powerful source of knowledge and hope.

I invite you to read this book as a companion on your own journey. May it inspire, encourage, and guide you as you find your own path to healing, growth, and self-discovery. It is my wish that this book will help bullied teenagers find their inner strength and believe in their own worth.

With sincere dedication,
Ria Berkhout

1

Hopeless

Max

It's three o'clock in the morning, and I still haven't fallen asleep. Today was one of the darkest days of my life. I can't bear this any longer. It has to stop, and it has to stop now. They're driving me insane.

I know it's all my fault. I'm fat, the fattest in the class. I hate my own body. Why am I like this? When I look at my sister, she's not chubby at all. She has a little belly, but that's it. It's nothing compared to my body. I understand perfectly why they bully me at school. They're right: I'm a big, fat pig.

The name-calling is one thing. It doesn't really hurt, but the pushing and pulling do. Especially on the stairs, when I walk down to English class and they deliberately trip me or knock things out of my hands. How many times have I had to pick up my scattered belongings from the stairs, only for them to step on my hand one after another? Actually, "stepping on it" is an understatement. Last week, someone stomped on my fingers so hard that one of them was bruised. It was so painful that until today I could barely use it to write.

This has to stop. I can't take it anymore. My stomach is in knots, and I feel like I'm going to be sick. The thought of going to school later is making me nauseous already. I don't want to go, I really don't. I can't handle another day of nightmares. The teasing, the sharp cutting remarks. The hurtful comments, the laughter and whispers behind my back. The hostile glances aimed at me. The physical violence. It's unbearable.

How can I make it stop? I just can't see a way out. I've been searching for a solution for so long, but I'm running out of ideas. I'm lost, I really am. How can I make them leave me alone? I feel so lonely, so incredibly alone, and completely disconnected from everyone else.

There's no point in talking to Mom and Dad; they don't listen anyway. They don't even see me, and if Mom does notice me, it's only to criticize. I can never do anything right. It's always like, "Max, hurry up; you're always so slow. What a useless person you are. It must be Max again; he's always so clumsy with his fat body." And it goes on like that. Just negativity, never a kind word or compliment.

The other day, I washed Mom's car. Sure, she had asked me a few times, but even then she couldn't say anything nice. All I heard was that I had to hurry up because she had to be on time for an appointment. Yes, suddenly she had to be on time for an appointment. She's always late everywhere.

I still remember all those minutes I spent waiting for her, being the last one to be picked up from school. I felt so insignificant. She had more important things to do than pick me up on time.

And Dad? He just sits in front of the TV every day. You can't disturb him because there's either breaking news or his favorite cop show. If you want to ask him something, it has to be during the commercial break, and even then, he doesn't really listen.

I don't want to continue like this. Life feels meaningless. I long for peace.

There's only one way out. Yes, there's only one way out.

2

The Departure

Helena

It's almost eleven o'clock at night as I drive out of Bordeaux. It has been a long day today. I teach businesses how to increase their productivity and revenue by working together as one team and striving for the same goal, whatever that may be. My passion lies in making employees feel like a part of the company, utilizing their true talents, and bringing out the best in themselves. They also learn the right communication techniques to persuade one another without resorting to pressure or manipulation. Sometimes it turns out that someone is not in the right position, and they can be transferred to another role, to their own satisfaction and that of everyone involved.

Today I had a great group to work with. They struggled a bit at first to let go and be themselves, but with the exercises I had prepared and a few jokes, the ice was quickly broken. Eventually, they worked hard as a unified group towards the goals they set for themselves and the company.

The evening ran late. Normally, I stop by ten o'clock at the latest, but tonight it was closer to eleven. After that, I still had over three and a half hours of driving back home. I had only driven about half a mile when I encountered dense fog with limited visibility. I could hardly see a hand in front of my face. "It's definitely going to take me an extra hour to get home," I think, unaware of what awaits me that night.

3

Car Trouble

I drive slowly through the dense fog. Why didn't I stay in the city and get a room there? Then I could have gotten a few hours of sleep at least. But I didn't feel like having to drive back home at five in the morning to prepare for my morning appointment.

If it continues like this the whole way, it's still going to be a very short night, no matter how you look at it.

A sigh of relief escapes me as the fog finally starts to thin out. I have better visibility now, and to my relief, I also have Internet connection again. I love listening to podcasts from inspiring people or interesting audiobooks on my phone while I drive. It motivates me and gives me positive energy, and I learn. At least I'm using my travel time productively.

What's that? I hear a strange noise and roll down my window. To my horror, my car is rattling. Please, don't let me down now. My plea doesn't work, because the car starts smoking too. Now things are serious. It's better if I stop, park on the side of the road, and call for roadside assistance. But where exactly am I? What was on the last sign I passed? They need to know my exact location to help me.

If I drive very slowly, maybe I'll reach the next sign. With sweaty hands, I continue slowly, afraid that it might damage my car. I don't know how many miles I've driven when I finally see a road marker. It's a good thing I didn't take the highway, but the local road. I pull over and call AAA, where I immediately get a helpful representative on the line.

He apologizes: it will take at least an hour and a half for roadside assistance to arrive because it's very busy tonight. Since I know I'm almost home, I agree with the man that I'll leave the key by the car and walk the rest of the way home. I look forward to a few more hours in my own bed, but that turns out to be wishful thinking.

4

A Strange Encounter

It's almost four o'clock as I walk into town. I'm tired and longing for my bed. I'm almost home; I just need to cross the old bridge. Normally, I can see my house clearly from this side, but it's hardly visible because of the fog. As I get closer, I see a figure sitting on the bridge railing. I wonder who's sitting there at this early hour. Probably a drunkard.

I scold myself for my own assumptions. Why does the person have to be a drunk? As I get closer, I see that it's a young person. It's hard to tell how old, but I estimate around fourteen. With that long hair, it could be a girl, but it appears to be a boy. I greet him kindly. He doesn't respond to my greeting. That's strange. Why would he be sitting there?

I come a bit closer and ask, "What are you doing here so early in the morning on the bridge? Don't you have a place to sleep?"

He turns towards me with a strange expression on his face. It's difficult to describe exactly what it is, but it certainly isn't happiness.

"Leave me alone," he snaps at me.

This isn't just a snappy answer. I can feel that there's more to it, because there's also sadness and despair in his voice.

"Isn't it very cold to sit here in the fog? Don't you have somewhere to go?"

I try to engage in a conversation, but I still don't get an answer. So I sit down next to him on the bridge railing and start talking to myself.

"What a night! I'm glad to take a seat. My car broke down, and I've just walked about six miles. And rest? No chance, because I have another appointment at ten o'clock."

I keep rambling on. I feel him starting to relax next to me.

"Do you think there are fish swimming here? Have you ever been fishing?" I ask. Without waiting for his answer, I continue. "I've never fished in this spot, but I have gone fishing in a big pond with friends. It was a lot of fun. I brought a big picnic basket with coffee, tea, sandwiches, apple pie, and other tasty treats." I chuckle at the memory. "The apple pie was almost the most important thing. Fishing's a fun activity, enjoyable and relaxing. You just need to have patience. My intention wasn't to catch a lot of fish, but to be in a relaxed environment."

He mumbles that he's never fished before. I continue my chatter about how much I enjoy the city and what I appreciate about it, but after a while, I start feeling so cold that I suggest we walk to my house. It's only a five-minute walk, and he can take shelter there and have something warm to drink.

He looks at me hesitantly, but I gently insist, "It's much more comfortable to sit by a warm stove."

Slowly, he first brings one leg and then the other to the other side of the bridge railing. Then he lowers himself down slowly. He is severely overweight. It's both impressive and sad to see a boy so heavy.

The hardest part is over. I pick up my things from the ground, and we walk to my house.

Upon arriving, I turn on the stove, then I invite him to sit at the table. Now I can see the wild, sad look in his eyes more clearly. The sweater he's wearing is torn and definitely a size too small.

"Would you like something to drink?" I ask.

"I'm not thirsty," he replies curtly. He clearly doesn't feel like talking.

"I'll make myself a cup of tea. It's no trouble to make something warm for you too," I insist.

"No, thank you."

I sense that he's uncomfortable. I'm not sure if he agrees with his own decision to come along.

"May I ask what you were doing on the bridge?" I say softly. "Or would you rather keep that to yourself? That's OK too, but is life so difficult right now that you can't see a way out?"

He looks surprised, confirming that I've hit the mark. I sit opposite him with my cup of tea and start telling him about my own life.

"You know, I remember the moment vividly. I was twelve years old, and I was standing in the garden of our new house. Suddenly, it hit me, and I thought, 'Is this life? Is this all there is? Isn't there more to it? We're born. We go to school. We take a job. We get married, have children, and then we die. I found it so pointless, and I felt incredibly empty. What's the meaning of life, then? Why am I here? If this is all there is, I'd rather leave.'

"I felt so empty. On top of that, I felt like a stranger. I was the only one in my family with red hair. I was tall and skinny, not fitting the ideal weight and height of that time. I believed wholeheartedly that I was adopted. I felt like the odd one out and a zombie in my own body. I wanted to make myself as small and inconspicuous as possible for my parents and the outside world, so they wouldn't have to be ashamed of such an ugly child.

"I felt like an ugly duckling. At school, I was bullied by other kids and called 'redhead.' I was also the only one with this hair color in school, and I felt lonely and different. But I didn't have the courage to end it all, even though I was utterly miserable and dragged myself through the days. The feeling lasted for years, but eventually, after finishing school and making friends elsewhere, the urge to end my life faded away.

"Later, I understood that it had to do with my thoughts about myself and the world. I learned that it's important to have a passion for life, to do things that I enjoy and that give me the energy to surround myself with like-minded people. I started ballroom dancing and discovered that I was good at it, and I enjoyed making my own clothes. Much later, I started reading inspiring books that showed me the meaning of life. Now I see the future in a more positive light. I am the master of my own life, and I don't fixate on the current situation but envision how I want my life to be. I take action to make it happen.

"Do you want to share the darkest incident from your life with me?" I ask him.

He bursts into tears and hides his face in his hands. I can see that he's struggling with his emotions. In our culture, it's still the case that a man, even a boy, is not allowed to cry. They're expected to be tough, especially in front of a stranger.

I let him know that I understand: "You're probably wondering, 'What does this woman think? That I'm going to share my life story with her? I don't even know her!'" I say. "But yes, I've also shared my childhood with you."

Tears stream down his cheeks, and when he speaks, his words are unintelligible.

"Take your time. I understand that you're feeling sad. Is life that difficult for you?" I ask.

"Yes," he replies between sobs. "I hate everything. I hate my body. I hate my life. I hate school. I hate the humiliation. I hate being at home. The bullying at school never stops. It goes on day and night; they never leave me alone, during the day at school and in the evenings on my phone. I can't take it anymore. It has to stop."

"Do you talk about this with your parents?" I ask.

"No," he answers, "it's pointless. They don't have time to listen to me. They'd rather watch their favorite TV shows or chat on social media. They don't even notice me, and if they do, it's only to criticize. I can never do anything right. They won't believe me, and they'll say, 'It will pass.' I don't want to bother them with what's happening at school, especially since Mom is often busy with my older sister."

"So you have an older sister? Do you have any other siblings?"

"Yes, another sister, who's much younger than me."

"How old is she?"

"She's almost eight months old and gets into everything," he answers with a deep sigh. "But my parents think she's so cute that they let her do anything and laugh at whatever she does. Then I have to clean up the mess because I'm older. Apparently I'm only good enough for that."

"That's not nice. Are you teaching your sister how to walk?"

"Oh, no. I'm not even allowed near her. They're so afraid that something might happen to her because I'm so clumsy."

"That's painful."

He nods, and I see deep sadness in his eyes.

After a short pause, I ask him, "Would you like me to talk to the school? Is there a teacher you trust?"

He looks at me with alarm. "Oh, no, don't talk to the school; that will only make it worse."

"Do you have friends at school?"

"Yes, one good friend."

"Can you talk to him?"

"No need to, because he sees what's happening."

"And he's never told an adult?"

"No," he says, "because my friend is afraid they'll target him too."

"Do you participate in any sports?"

"No. With a body like mine, what do you think?"

"What could make you feel better and make the bullying stop?" I ask.

"I have no idea. Of course, I want it to stop, and I want it to stop now."

"If you want, I can help you look at yourself in a different way and talk and think about yourself differently. I can teach you techniques to stand up for yourself so that you'll at least feel better about yourself. Another solution is to talk to a child psychologist, but you'd have to discuss it with your parents first. What do you think about that?"

"I don't know," he says hesitantly. "Talking to my parents is absolutely pointless."

"I understand, but if you're willing and open to it, I can help you with some exercises that have helped me. These are things that are important to know and understand, things you don't learn at school. They are universal laws, like the law of attraction, which I can delve into another time. But there are a lot of interesting universal laws."

"What are universal laws?"

"One law you know very well is the law of gravity. It determines that when you jump off a tall building, you always go down. You never fly upwards. It always works, with no exceptions, whether you believe in it or not. I wouldn't try to see if there might be an exception to the rule," I add with a smile.

"Due to the earth's gravity, you will always come down sooner or later. It's a great advantage to understand how the laws of nature work so that you become aware of how they operate and can use them to your advantage rather than your disadvantage. By the way, what's your name?"

"Max."

"That's a great name. Did you know it's a very powerful name? *Max* is a shortened form of *Maximilian, Maximus, Maxentius*, or *Maxwell*. The first three names come from the Latin word *maximus*, which means *the greatest*. Not great in size, but great in deeds," I add. "You can look up the name on the Internet."

"Wow, no, I didn't know that." I see him sit up a little straighter.

"My name is Helena," I said. "I'm originally from the Netherlands and have been living here in France for twenty-three years now."

I look at the clock with a start.

"Max, it's almost five o'clock! What are you going to do? I would like to get a few more hours of sleep before my appointment."

Max looks at me in silence for a moment.

"I'm going home," he says. "When can I come back to talk to you again?"

"Send me a message. I have a lot of appointments scheduled for this week, but I will definitely find a moment when we can continue our conversation."

I give him my phone number. As he walks towards the door, he turns around.

"Why do you live here in the middle of France?"

I burst into laughter. "You've got it right. I am and will always be an outsider. Or, as we say in Dutch, a *vreemde eend in de bijt*—a strange duck in the flock."

5

Hope

Max

Slowly I walk back home, reflecting on the whole incident. What a night! Who would have expected this turn of events? Certainly not me, but I'm glad it happened. I see light at the end of the tunnel again, thanks to the conversation with this intriguing woman. She understands me and knows what I'm talking about. I can undoubtedly learn a lot from her.

It's about a fifteen-minute walk from her house to mine. It's a good thing it's still early. Everyone is still asleep, and no one will have noticed my absence at home. Later, I'll dive into my bed and pretend nothing happened, but my worldview has completely flipped. I have hope again.

I breathe in the fresh, damp morning air. It's still misty, but the fog is gradually lifting. Suddenly, I feel very tired. I'll go to bed early tonight, and maybe I should also stop checking my social media in the evenings. I pick up my pace. I'm almost there.

Oops! I hear noise coming from my house. It can't be that the baby is awake so early. I climb up through the shed and enter my bedroom window, just as my mother opens the door.

"Max, can you come help? Your sister is sick; she's thrown up everywhere. Her bed needs changing, and the floor needs to be mopped."

A new day starts early. She doesn't even notice that I'm still wearing my clothes.

6

Reunion

Helena

A few days later, I receive a message from Max. He asks when he can come over. I quickly arrange a meeting with him.

He sits across from me at the table. He looks tired and has the eyes of a frightened rabbit.

"Would you like something to drink?" I ask.

"No, thank you; I'm not thirsty," he replies.

"You don't have to be thirsty to have something to drink," I smile. "I'm making myself a hot chocolate; can I make you one too?"

"No, thank you, really."

As I sit down, I ask him, "How was your week? Do you want to talk about it, or should we dive right into your biggest problem? I want to understand what's going on."

"I want to talk about the bullying at school," Max says. "That's my biggest problem, and it's absolutely unbearable. I thought it would go away, but it's only getting worse. I want it to stop, but I don't know how. I have nightmares, especially when I read the messages on my phone at night. They make me sick. I'm going crazy from the gossip behind my back, the photos secretly taken and edited. Kids I don't even know look at me strangely and laugh at me. I don't even know which way to look anymore. I feel so alone and excluded."

He bursts into a fit of intense crying. All the pent-up sadness comes pouring out. It takes at least fifteen minutes for him to start calming down.

"It has to stop," he sobs. "Every night, those nightmares. Sometimes I decide not to go to sleep at all, but then the night feels so long, and I keep worrying. In fact, that's even worse. I lie there, worrying about what might happen at school the next day and how I can prevent it."

"Max," I ask, "can you tell me exactly what happens and when it started?"

"I don't remember when the bullying started exactly. I think I was around eleven years old when boys in my class started making jokes about my overweight body.

"Actually, I found it quite normal for them to make a comment because they're right: I am a fat pig. I didn't know what to say in response. But at some point, the bullying became worse, and they started being even more unpleasant to me. They took pleasure in targeting me with biting remarks, picking fights, and damaging my belongings."

Max continues hesitantly.

"Since then, they snatch my schoolbag and throw it from one person to another, so I have to chase after it while they jeer at me saying, 'Hey, Piggy, you need to be *here*.' They throw my bag amidst loud laughter and cheering to the next person, making snorting noises in the process. Or they empty it and tear apart my things. My homework often bears the brunt of it. And every time I have to gather all my belongings, they sarcastically laugh, most of the time adding a punch, kick, or shove as a bonus. Often this makes me late for class, resulting in comments or extra assignments from the teacher. Of course, I can't tell them the truth, or I'll be torn apart.

"They've even thrown my backpack in the toilet or had a few guys urinate on it. I no longer use the school restroom because I'm certain something will happen to my schoolbag, or I'll be beaten up. I often stand there with tears in my eyes, but I hide them to avoid making the situation worse. At some point, they started giving me a slap on the back when I stood in the hallway waiting for the next class or walking up the stairs. And it wasn't just one person, but the whole group, one after another, about ten guys, whenever they had the chance. They always did it discreetly, so the rest of my class and the teacher wouldn't notice. By the end of the day, the pain in my back becomes almost unbearable."

"Sometimes they kick me or trip me. They challenge me to fight on the school playground. Of course, I always lose, because they outnumber me. I often come home with torn clothes, and then I get scolded by my mother. Two years ago, they took away my new winter coat. I searched for it everywhere, in and around school, but never found it again. In the mornings, I would leave quickly so my mother wouldn't see me without a coat, or I would make up an excuse. And that winter happened to be one of the coldest winters in the last fifty years. After walking to school for fifteen minutes, I would be so frozen and stiff that I had trouble sitting down in the first class.

"I have lost many clothing items like this, which I can't tell my family about. Only when I come home with visible bruises, a remark is made, but then I always have to come up with an excuse."

He remains silent to catch his breath. "I can't take it anymore," he sighs. "In the school cafeteria," he continues, sobbing, "no one wants to sit next to me anymore, and when I serve my food, I have to be careful not to have someone bump into my arm or purposely collide with my tray, causing everything to spill onto the floor.

"Eating there has become a nightmare, so three months ago, I decided to stop going there. Instead, I wander the streets until it's time for my next class."

"What do you have for lunch then?" I inquire.

"Sometimes I have money to buy a sandwich from the bakery, but most days, I go without eating and endure the gnawing hunger in my stomach."

"Hasn't any teacher ever noticed what's happening? And how does the cafeteria staff react?" I ask. "Surely it must be visible what's happening."

"I don't know if they see it. They're so busy preparing food and refilling the big bins. And on the school playground, it always happens when I'm out of sight of the teachers."

"But there are other kids who see it, right?"

"Yes, but they don't say anything. They're afraid that they'll be bullied themselves."

"Yes, I remember what it's like to be bullied, how sad, powerless, and alone you feel," I reply. "Shall we see together what you can do about it?"

Max nods resignedly.

"Max," I continue, "you just said they bully you because of your fat body. But how do you see yourself? Do you think you are fat? Or do you accept yourself the way you are?"

"What a weird question," Max says, horrified. "Of course I don't accept being so fat. I hate my body. It's awful to be this fat and inconvenient. I'm constantly out of breath. I can barely tie my shoelaces, and everything wobbles on me."

"When did you start gaining weight?" I ask.

"When I look at old photos of myself," Max replies, "I think I was about seven years old when I started growing and gradually became fatter."

"Do you have any idea what could be the reason for that?" I ask him.

"Not really," he says. "I can't remember changing my eating habits. But now that I'm so fat, I'm constantly hungry and eat whatever is available: chocolate, cookies, candies, desserts. I even eat frozen crepes without thawing them. I have such an urge to eat all day, and it doesn't matter what it is."

"When you have such a binge eating episode, do you feel guilty afterwards?"

"Sometimes," he replies. "My weight is the biggest issue after the bullying."

"Max," I ask, "would you like to work on both things at the same time? Achieving your ideal weight and finding your place in a group of friends who respect you?"

Max's face brightens up.

"If that could happen!"

"I don't have a magic solution for you," I continue. "And it will take time. But everything is possible if you want it. It's a matter of taking baby steps. The first thing you need is to *decide* that you want this. *Believe* that you can do it. And *take action* to make it happen."

I look at him intently. "Can you make those promises to yourself? Because, remember, you're not doing it for me, but for yourself."

"Yes," Max says. "I'll do anything as long as I don't have to starve."

I burst out laughing.

"Of course not. That would be too dangerous for someone in their growing years like you. Instead, we're going to focus on what we can add."

"Really?" Max asks, wide-eyed.

"Yes," I say. "We'll add some exercise, because the body is meant to move."

That clearly doesn't appeal to Max as much.

"Max," I continue, "we've gone through a lot of emotions. Shall we stop for today?"

"Please," Max replies. "But can I come back on Tuesday?"

"I'm available on Tuesday afternoon after two o'clock. What's a good time for you?"

"Three o'clock, please."

"Great. See you on Tuesday, Max."

7

Thoughts and Habits: What Do You Say to Yourself?

On that Tuesday, we continue our conversation.

"Well," I say, "it's time to work on your self-confidence and self-image. Does that sound like a good plan?"

"I think so," says Max.

"Let me start by explaining what our thoughts and habits are and what consequences they can have. You'll discover that you can change your thoughts about yourself and situations. You say, 'I am fat,' but you are not fat. You simply have a fat body. It's like saying, 'I am a hand.' You are not a hand, but you have a hand. Or 'I am a victim.' But you are not a victim; you have had a victimizing experience. Do you understand what I mean? Because if you grasp that difference, then you're already halfway there."

I see Max pondering over what I'm saying.

"As long as you believe that you are your body, it's difficult to change it. It's important to separate the two and step out of the victim role."

Max nods, indicating that he understands.

"So you are not your body, just as you are not your hand or your foot. The next question, of course, is, who is Max then? If you are not your body, what are you?"

I don't wait for his answer but continue: "You are a spiritual being, living in a material or physical body. You're whole and complete, which is why you can say, 'I am funny,' 'I am brilliant,' 'I am smart.' Because everyone is whole and complete."

Max's eyes widen.

"I know," I say, smiling at the memory. "I remember the first time I heard this. I absolutely disagreed with it. I felt far from whole and complete. In fact, very few people truly believe this. It has nothing to do with vanity or anything like that. Vanity is just an attitude of someone who doesn't believe in themselves. But if you truly believe in yourself, you don't need that. Many people spend their whole lives playing the role they learned as young children, as a survival mechanism. But as we grow older, we can take care of ourselves and love ourselves, and we don't actually need that role anymore. Are you still following me, Max?"

He nods in agreement.

"The role you play is related to how you think about yourself or how you perceive yourself," I continue. "You might wonder how we take on roles.

"That brings me to consciousness and subconsciousness. Many studies, including those by Freud and Jung, have been conducted to understand our thinking and response systems. What emerges from these studies is that until the age of seven, the subconscious mind is wide open. We absorb everything said and done in our environment. It's stored in our subconsciousness."

"What do you mean by that?" Max asks.

"Let's compare ourselves to a computer. You are a computer, complete with everything. The hard drive represents the subconscious mind. It accepts everything you put on it. Consciousness is the software: the programs you write for your computer. You add something or replace something on your hard drive. The computer is a unity, just like humans, and all computers are connected through the Internet, where data is stored and messages are distributed.

"The same applies to humans. We are all interconnected. We are part of a collective energy, like the Internet. We are all pure energy. Einstein discovered that years ago. When we break down the molecules of our body into smaller and smaller elements, all that remains is energy. Energy also has a frequency, but we'll talk more about that later."

I'm curious if he is still following. "Can you relate, Max, to this analogy?"

"Yes, I think I understand," he replies.

"As children, we unconsciously absorb all input from our environment. You can see aspects of children's environment reflected in their characteristics, for example, how a father or mother behaves, but it can also be an older sibling or someone else important in their life. When we're young, we're like parrots: we copy and store data. That's when we form a self-image.

"To change something about yourself and your life, you need to put new data on your hard drive. You have to overwrite the old data. Consciousness resists: it wants everything to stay the same. That's why a voice in your head (also known as the ego) tells you, 'Don't bother; everything is fine as it is.' The ego doesn't want chaos and confusion because a new thought or habit doesn't align with what is stored in your subconscious mind (your old program).

"Changing your life happens in two ways. It can occur through a significant or traumatic event or through repetition."

"What do you mean by that?" Max asks me with a furrowed brow.

"I'm referring to an event such as 9/11, for example. Many people who experienced trauma during that time no doubt unconsciously decided in a fraction of a second that it's unsafe to live in a big city or a tall building. They have overwritten their hard drive with this new thought that they are not safe there. If this new thought is repeated frequently, it becomes a new truth. And you react based on that new truth.

"Such an unconscious decision has significant consequences. The fear of insecurity is deeply ingrained in their hard drive. In addition to feeling uncomfortable or fearful, they may develop symptoms associated with the feeling. They might experience agoraphobia or be unable to enter tall buildings. The voice in their head will keep telling them that things are not safe.

"I'm telling you all this because it's important to understand how this unconscious mechanism works. When you want to lose weight, you're not just working with your body but also with your mind. The first step is to detach from the 'I am' thought. Then, with your thoughts, your consciousness—that is, your software—you can give instructions to your body. Your body doesn't do anything on its own. You control it with your mind. You can tell your body what is good for it and what is not. *The mind is the boss, and the body must obey.*

"It sounds simple, but there's one catch: we have programmed ourselves, so we need to examine our programs. What have we, consciously or unconsciously, put on our hard drive? The program is what we do automatically, the habits we have copied from what we observed around us, the conclusions we have drawn from various situations, and the thoughts and habits we have adopted.

"I mentioned earlier that we develop habits by repeating thoughts. We do so automatically. We have put our body on autopilot, just like when we learned to walk. When we started standing up (by copying the people around us) and took the first steps, we had to concentrate and practice repeatedly. Over time, walking became automatic. We no longer have to think about how to put one foot in front of the other.

"Let me give you a simple exercise that will allow you to experience giving commands to your body and see how it reacts when you do something different from what you're used to. I'll grab a sheet of paper, a pen, and the first book I see lying around for you. Now write down four lines from the first chapter of this book."

Max hastily writes down the lines in messy handwriting.

"Now write down the same four lines with your other hand."

Max looks at me with wide eyes. "But I can't write with my other hand!"

"That's what you think. Give it a try."

He starts working on it, and soon he starts groaning and struggling. The letters are unrecognizable. It takes him four times as long to get the lines on paper.

"What I'm trying to demonstrate with this exercise," I tell him, "is that we have trained ourselves, through repetitive practice, to write legibly with our dominant hand. If you were to repeat this exercise every day for ninety days, you would program yourself to write legibly with your other hand as well. But you have to give that command to your body. It doesn't do it on its own.

"As for our belief system, we have both positive and negative thinking patterns stored on our hard drive, our subconscious. These patterns are also known as *paradigms*.

"Negative thinking patterns can include statements such as: 'I'm always late for everything.' 'When I come home from school, I raid the fridge.' 'I need chocolate to feel good.' 'I only do my homework at the last minute.' 'I belittle others with violence.' 'I use foul language and need to appear tough, or else I won't fit in with the group.' 'I get sick every winter.' These are deeply ingrained thoughts."

I take a sip of my tea.

"How do you find out about these?" Max asks.

"By observing what happens in your life. Are you satisfied with the results of your habits or not?" I reply. "Do they take you where you want to go? Do they give you what you want to have or be? Think about your weight. To achieve your ideal weight, you must first examine your thoughts and habits related to eating. What do you eat? In what quantities and at what times? Under what circumstances? What triggers make you eat or snack?

"By answering these questions, you gain insight into your own eating pattern. When you understand how you work, you know what new commands you can give to your body by changing a thought first. *The thought changes a habit, and the habit changes your program—your paradigm. As a result, you change the outcome.*

"When I want to study a habit, such as an eating habit, for a longer period of time, say a month, I carry a small notebook with me and write down everything I eat and at what time, even the smallest thing. I do it immediately after eating, and I also note my mood."

I add with a laugh, "You'll see: at some point, you'll think twice before putting something in your mouth because you'll have to take out that notebook again to write it down. So it already helps you eat less. As for your eating habits, Max, I recommend that from now on, for one week, without changing anything in your eating pattern, you write down everything you eat. And by everything, I mean *everything*. This is to make you broadly aware of what you eat. The next time you come, bring your list, and we'll go through it together to see what your habits and eating patterns are. What do you think of that? Are you open to doing it?"

"Yes, of course. It sounds very straightforward."

"OK, let's stop for today. How did you experience it, Max? I know it was quite a lot to take in, but I tried to explain it as simply as possible."

"It *was* a lot. I'll let it sink in. Thank you, Helena. See you next time."

8

Accepting Yourself

Max calls me the next morning at nine o'clock. He has the afternoon off at two o'clock because a class has been canceled. He asks if I have time to talk then. I understand that Max is eager to continue working on stepping out of his current pattern. I reschedule an appointment on the other line and tell him it's fine.

Max arrives in the afternoon in the pouring rain. After his coat and sweater are in the dryer, he sits wrapped in a brown blanket on the beige leather couch, and we continue our conversation.

"Max, we're going to continue working on the image you have of yourself—what you say to yourself—and *accepting yourself*."

He looks at me with wide eyes. "What do you mean by 'accepting yourself'? How can I accept myself? No way! We've already talked about that, about this big, fat body of mine."

"I understand," I continue. "But there is no other way. *Accepting yourself, not just your body, is one of the most important things you can do*. From there, you can work on yourself safely. In other words, we start with the end goal in mind and accept the situation as it is today. That means accepting your body as it is now. Acceptance doesn't mean justifying it or staying stuck in it. It's more about telling yourself that it is what it is, and it was created by past thoughts and habits, and telling yourself, 'Today I am creating new habits and thoughts for my future.'

"Let's compare it to going on vacation. Imagine this: life is going smoothly, everything is OK, but then you decide that you want to go on vacation—to meet new people, explore cities, or whatever it may be. You start preparing. You think about where you would like to go, and in your mind, you're already traveling and envisioning different things. Then you decide where and when you want to go, and you look forward to it. You feel happy and excited.

"With the destination in mind, you start figuring out how to get there. What is needed to reach your destination? What mode of transportation do you need: a bike, car, bus, train, plane, or boat? If it's far away, you book the transportation. You enjoy doing it because you already feel in the vacation spirit. Then you check what documents are required: a passport, visa, travel insurance? Is your health insurance in order? You check and make sure everything is in place if something is missing.

"Furthermore, you enjoy learning more about the destination, and you do some research. You go shopping to buy vacation clothes. You are excited that the time is almost here, and you can already envision yourself wearing the clothes you buy. A day or several days before, you start packing your suitcase or backpack, and you feel thrilled that you're almost going on vacation. You still feel happy and excited about the prospect. You have already experienced your entire vacation in advance. You feel happy and excited, as if you were already there. This is the big trick that allows you to change your life.

"Now let's talk about your weight. The journey to your desired weight is exactly the same as going on vacation."

"You must be joking," Max says indignantly.

"No, you're doing exactly the same thing as when you go on vacation. You can have the same anticipation in planning and organizing. See your ideal weight as your vacation. Thinking about it gives you a sense of excitement and happiness. You can already envision yourself at your ideal weight. You feel fantastic, healthy, and slim. You hear people complimenting how great you look.

"Then comes the preparation for your destination. What kind of food do you eat—what products, what quantities? What time do you eat? In what time frame do you want to lose how many pounds? Stick to reasonable standards. In short, you consider everything to bring you to your end goal. Throughout, you constantly hold the image in your mind of being slim, and you feel excited and happy. You already have the feeling you desire.

"You feel good on the day you decide to go on vacation. That means you feel good about yourself on that day. In other words, you accept yourself exactly as you are at that moment, not only when you have reached your end goal. Because if you say, 'I will only accept myself and love myself when I have lost weight,' you'll get stuck.

"First, you have to determine how many pounds you need to lose to be happy. Let's say, for example, ten pounds. What happens when those ten pounds are gone? Then you start criticizing your body again. Maybe you find your stomach too flabby, and so on. Do you understand? There is no end to it. It will never be good enough. That's why people are often frustrated: because they seek feeling good outside of themselves. It's always in the future. And the future never arrives. So acceptance of yourself is the key to change.

"At the same time you're working on losing weight, you overwrite your inner program with positive statements that support you. They are called *affirmations*. An affirmation is a confirmation that you repeat as much as possible every day. You can say to yourself, 'I fully accept myself exactly as I am, and every day I become slimmer and slimmer. It's a pleasure to have such a slim, beautiful, healthy, well-functioning body.'

"By the way, take a moment to think about how beautiful your body is right now. It breathes without you having to think about it. Your heart pumps blood around. You have two legs that take you everywhere. Two arms to embrace with. Two hands to create. See how beautiful it is."

"Yes, this does give a different perspective on my body," Max mumbles to himself.

"To summarize: accept yourself exactly as you are right now, including your excess weight. Keep your end goal in mind, and work backward from there. Consider what you need to do to achieve it. What steps do you need to take? And start looking forward to the end result. Because, as I said before, if you don't accept yourself as you are right now, there will always be a reason for being dissatisfied with yourself.

"I know all about it," I laugh. "Because I used to be a champion at criticizing myself, and I felt miserable. I carried around a sense of inferiority for years. As a young child, I programmed myself to always feel I was less than others. I constantly criticized myself and felt ugly. Even if someone said I was a beautiful woman, I would only briefly feel the compliment, and then my own belief system would take over again.

"It wasn't until I started working on myself—disconnecting my thoughts from who I thought I was and replacing my limiting beliefs with what I truly am—that I began to appreciate and accept myself. I became my own best friend and gained confidence in life.

"My world also changed. It was one of the major breakthroughs in my life. My world is now full of loving, helpful people. I'm happy with my beautiful life, grateful for all the abundance. My happiness comes from within. I don't depend on circumstances or what people do or say. That's the best feeling there is. I am free.

"But I digress. Let's get back to your weight loss. I told you that it's important to exercise. What do you think about going for a run?"

"Running? But that's impossible for me," Max exclaims in horror.

"Impossible is only impossible if you think it's impossible."

"Helena, let's be honest. Even walking is challenging for me. How do you expect me to run with my large body?"

"By using baby steps."

Max looks at me with wide eyes. "What do you mean by baby steps?"

"You have to build something up, bit by bit. Of course you can't run five miles tomorrow. You have to build up to that. That's what I mean by baby steps. You start with a small loop, for example, half a mile. You run at your own pace, stop when you can't go on, then you continue walking. Once you have your breath under control again, you run a little more.

"Be enthusiastic about every step you run. Think of it like a vacation: your end goal. Every day, try to run a bit longer until you can do one mile in one go. Do it at your own pace, even if it takes three months. The goal is to enjoy it. Then you build up to two loops and so on and so forth. In one or two years, you'll run a marathon," I add with a laugh.

"You see, everything is possible. How do you think top athletes do it? It takes years of training. Exercise is very good for your body, because you breathe deeper and your heart pumps faster, which brings more oxygen into your blood. You'll find that it's easier to lose weight with a combination of exercise and nutrition. You'll feel better about yourself. It's about self-worth, self-respect, self-confidence. Everything is interconnected."

"All right, I'll give it a try. The way you describe it sounds very simple."

I nod encouragingly at him.

"It's time to wrap up. Let's delve deeper into your nutrition next time. But don't worry: we'll take baby steps with that too. Start by keeping track of what you eat and promise me that you'll refrain from criticizing yourself while doing it. It's purely for observation."

9

Nutrition: What Do You Put in Your Mouth?

It's a beautifully sunny day. I'm sitting in the garden, enjoying the tranquility. As happens every year, a bird has built its nest under the roof tiles of my house, and I can hear the little chicks making more and more noise. Soon they will take flight.

I've just closed my eyes to focus more on their chirping when I hear the garden gate. Someone is coming. Suddenly Max is standing in front of me.

"Hi," he says. "I was in the area and thought I'd check if you're home. Is this a good time?"

"I have half an hour, then I need to prepare for my next appointment. How has it been going?" I ask. "Have you started writing down everything you eat?"

"Yes, I asked my mom for a notebook the next day. I didn't tell her why, because she doesn't care what I do. It's like you said: I have to do this for myself."

"You're right, but it's also important that your mother knows about it so she can support you."

"Support me?" Max exclaims indignantly. "Don't make me laugh. She's been complaining about everything all day long. I don't want to burden her with this too!"

"OK," I say with a sigh, letting it go. I can't change his mind right now. "Let's look at your list. What do you think of it? How was your week? It's been ten days since we last saw each other."

"I was shocked," says Max, "by what I eat in a day. I had absolutely no awareness."

"Yes, it really opens your eyes," I reply. "I see," looking at his list, "that you're a big fan of pasta. And you eat very irregularly."

"I told you, I haven't been eating at the school cafeteria for three months. Sometimes I have enough money for a chocolate pastry from the bakery. If not, I raid the fridge when I come home from school."

"Don't they notice that at home, Max? The rapid decrease in food in the fridge?"

"My mother says that we eat her out of house and home, but she thinks it's because we're growing. She and Dad also regularly go to the fridge to grab something."

"I understand, Max," I say. "You should know that I'm not a dietitian, but over the course of my life, I've done research on what is good for my body and what isn't. I know how food affects us and how to change my own eating patterns without harming my body or starving myself.

"Of course, everyone is different. It also depends on the type of person we are. Some people feel great eating raw vegetables, while others prefer warm meals or avoid meat because of personal or religious beliefs. I feel most comfortable with warm meals, and I eat almost everything, except for a few things that I genuinely don't like, just like everyone else.

"I'll explain the basics of nutrition to you. You need to watch out for carbohydrates. They cause a yo-yo effect in your body by rapidly raising your blood sugar levels. They give you a feeling of satisfaction, but later, when your blood sugar levels drop to the lowest point, you quickly feel hungry again, even though your food hasn't been fully digested. If you eat again quickly at that point, the undigested food is stored in fat cells. You end up in a vicious cycle where more and more fat is stored in fat cells.

"The foods I'm referring to are potatoes, white rice, and refined grain products like white bread. This also includes anything related to bread, cookies, and cake. If you want to lose weight, these are the products you need to watch closely. It's best to eliminate them completely for now until you reach your desired weight.

"In your case, it's not just the carbohydrates, but also the high number of calories you consume, primarily from refined sugars.

"I've already mentioned that we're going to add things. Back then, I was talking about physical exercise, but now it's about vegetables and fruits."

Max makes a disgusted face. "I have no appetite for that at all."

"I understand, looking at your list," I smile. "But maybe you haven't learned to eat them or maybe you don't know their value. With fruit, you always have to be a bit cautious, because some fruits, like bananas, can have a lot of sugars. But you can eat several apples. It's easy. You can eat them wherever you want: just wash the peel and take a bite.

"Vegetables have comparatively few calories," I continue, "so you can eat a lot of them to feel full and satisfied. It's important not to feel hungry. If you're constantly hungry, it's difficult to change your eating habits, and you might fall back into your old patterns. It takes perseverance, because changing an eating habit takes at least thirty days."

"That long?" Max says, surprised.

"Unfortunately, it will take even longer for you, because I see that you consume a lot of things with high sugar content, like chocolate pastries, cookies, cake, chocolate, and candies. You also drink a lot of soda. Consuming a lot of sugar is like smoking: it's an addiction that you need to overcome. The withdrawal process takes about six weeks."

Max looks dejected. "All those delicious things."

"But," I continue, "if you know the harmful effects of sugars—that it has been scientifically proven to deplete calcium in the bones—it can be a good motivation to eliminate as much sugar as possible. After all, don't you want to age healthily? It's also been discovered that prolonged sugar overdose can cause cancer and heart conditions. Sugar has a fundamental effect on our ability to form new memories and learn new information. And glucose affects insulin levels in the body. As a result, sugar spikes can cause feelings of anxiety and sudden mood swings. When we consume too much of this substance, it will lead to constant feelings of hunger. This is directly related to obesity and overweight.

"Look it up on the Internet: the harmful effects of sugar. I advise you to research everything I'm saying on your own. That way, you can draw your own conclusions.

"I don't see water on your list," I continue. "Don't you drink water at all? Only soda?"

"Water is for fish," Max says firmly.

"That's true, but it's also for you. We are made up of 70 percent water, and it needs to be replenished, so drinking water is important, and it contains no calories. Especially in the beginning, make sure to drink enough water to flush waste products out of your body quickly. I think a liter a day should be sufficient. Don't overdo it, and definitely don't drink a whole liter at once if you didn't have time to drink any water during the day. Your kidneys won't appreciate that.

"You'll see that when you add water to your daily habits, you'll have less desire for soda, because you'll be less thirsty. And water gives you energy."

I decide to involve him more in the process. "Max, how do you think you can start eating more vegetables and fruits?" He shrugs. "I could eat an apple at 10 a.m. and another one at 4 p.m., but as for vegetables, I'm not sure. I'll have to think about that."

"That's a good idea. But if you find it difficult to add them, for example, in the first few days, have a chocolate pastry and an apple, then on the third day, have half a chocolate pastry and an apple, and on the fifth day, just have your apple. Do it in a way that feels best for you. I told you last time that it's best to take baby steps. You need to see these new eating habits as the foundation for the rest of your life. It's not something temporary; you're creating a new healthy lifestyle. It's like building a house. We start with the foundation."

I am very happy that Max isn't resisting my advice, but it won't be easy for him to put everything into practice, so I summarize it for him: "For now, let's avoid potatoes, grains, or rice. And if you do have grains and rice, ask your family to switch to whole grain varieties. A good daily foundation consists of meat, fish, eggs, vegetables, fruits, and nuts. Freshly squeezed juice is fine, but avoid prepackaged fruit juices, as they are too concentrated and contain a lot of sugar. Also, try to avoid pork. Although it's rich in protein, it's also high in saturated fats, which can increase your risk of heart disease, obesity, and other long-term health issues.

"Vegetables are always good. Be moderate with cow's milk products, because cow's milk is meant for calves to grow into adult cows, and we humans are not exactly the same. You certainly don't want to grow into a cow, do you?"

"No," Max laughs. "I'm already a pig, and that's bad enough." We both burst into laughter.

"Milk products from goats and sheep are better. You can also try soy products. They make me gassy, so I don't eat them.

They are relatively heavy for the body to digest, but they are a good alternative to meat, just like legumes, all kinds of beans, red and green lentils, chickpeas, and yellow or green peas. These have slightly less nutritional value, so if you have no issues with eating meat, I recommend continuing to do so. Your body can digest sixty to 100 grams of meat per day. If you eat much more, it stays in your body longer and starts to decay. Have you ever smelled spoiled meat? That says enough.

"I suggest taking about a week to figure out what works best for you in terms of what to eat and when. In any case, try to finish your meals by 7 p.m. to allow your food time to digest before sleeping. Don't rush, and don't go to extremes, because that's not sustainable. And talk about it at home.

"Always remember, Max: baby steps, baby steps, and more baby steps. Slow and steady wins the race.

"I know it's a lot of information, Max, and I still remember how challenging it was when I decided to cut out refined sugars and had to figure out what I could eat. In the beginning, I was very frustrated. I would walk into a supermarket, couldn't find anything, and walked out again. It's truly a search, because sugar is present in so many products. Later, I realized it's also used as a preservative. The only solution was to look at brands that I normally never bought. In your case, it's a bit more challenging, because you don't do the grocery shopping yourself. How can you ensure that your parents buy products without sugar?"

Max furrows his eyebrows. "I could start by looking at the ingredients of the products I usually eat at home. I can go to the supermarket to search for healthier options and make a grocery list for home."

"Good idea," I nod. "There are also apps on your phone nowadays that indicate the ingredients of a product. I discovered that it's best to cook for myself, and luckily, I was already doing that. It could become a new hobby for you! What's important is being aware of what you eat and making choices based on that. But the quantity and size of the portions you serve are also important. When I wanted to lose weight, using a smaller plate helped, because it made my plate look fuller. Sometimes you have to pull out some tricks to fool yourself. But if it helps, why not? It's for a good cause."

I glance at my watch and see that it's almost time for my appointment. Max looks flushed. He has taken a lot of notes in a notebook and now looks thoughtful.

"Can you make use of this?"

"Yes, absolutely. I have written down a lot of what you said, and I'll see how I can apply it."

"Good. Let's stop for today. Do you have time tomorrow at half past twelve? I'll prepare a healthy lunch for you, and we can continue talking about bullying. Until what time are you free?"

"I only have English class at three o'clock," he says, and I see his eyes light up at the mention of lunch.

"Fantastic. Then we have plenty of time to eat and talk at leisure."

I see a glimmer of hope in his eyes again, and I'm glad I can make a difference for him. Life is full of surprises. Ask, and you shall receive. You just have to be open to receiving it; that's the big secret to getting what you want. Max was looking for a solution, and I could help him with that. Not that I have all the answers, but I could at least set him on the right path. He'll have to do the rest himself. No one can do it for him.

My eyes follow him as he closes the garden gate behind him, and I hear his footsteps fading away in the distance. It's time for me to get ready for my next appointment.

10

Lunch

The next day is radiant. It's still chilly, but the sun is doing its best to evaporate the dew. It promises to be warm. The garden smells delightful, and everything looks wonderfully refreshed. There are frogs in the lake near my house, but I only hear them croaking when the wind blows from a certain direction. This morning, that happens to be the case, and I enjoy it. It's so different from the end of the day, when the sun's heat has made my garden dry and arid.

I decide to have lunch under the old lime tree, which is my favorite spot in the whole garden. It's impressively large and provides ample shade. I spend a lot of time there. It inspires me when I write my books or prepare lessons for companies. On one side, I've set up a table with a few chairs, and on the other side, there's a cozy bench with comfortable, brightly colored cushions that you can sink into.

I gaze at the tree and drift off into reverie. How old could it be, and who planted it? And why specifically there? Lime trees can live for a long time. They say 400 to 600 years.

The only history I know about my tree is that it served as a landmark for the English planes during World War II. It was marked on their maps. I'm quite proud of that. Imagine if my tree could tell all the things it has witnessed: budding loves, a first kiss, a newborn baby gazing at the rustling leaves in its crib.

In the time of the Celts and the ancient Germans, the lime tree was revered. It was seen as a sacred tree that protected houses, churches, and water sources. Later, in the Middle Ages, justice was delivered under it, and marriages were concluded there. What might my tree have experienced? I inhale the delightful sweet scent of its flowers. Just one more month, and I can pick them. I'll dry them and make herbal tea with them in the winter. They help me sleep soundly, but they have many other beneficial properties too. Has anyone ever written a song about my lime tree?

Lost in my thoughts, I hear the church bell chime twelve in the distance. I snap out of my reverie: it's time for action, because Max will be at my doorstep in half an hour.

It's half past twelve when Max arrives, his face red. With tears in his eyes and out of breath, he stands before me gasping for air.

"Hi," he says barely audible.

"Max, did you have to rush like that? But bravo, you're right on time." I hear my antique clock in the parlor strike the half-hour.

"I had plenty of time to be here before half past twelve," he pants, "but they were waiting for me and ambushed me. I'm afraid to look at my legs tonight because I think I've got a lot more bruises."

Deep inside me, there is great sadness, but that won't help Max. I need to stay focused on the end result—what we want to achieve, his goal. Max wants love, harmony, acceptance, and respectful friends. That's where my focus should be, not on the current situation. It's merely a consequence of what he has created in the past.

Once we've settled into the comfortable chairs, we start our lunch. Max has had time to calm down while I set the table. I've kept everything in the fridge until the last moment, so it would be nice and cold. He clearly enjoys the cold chicken I roasted yesterday, and I'm a fan of vegetables, so they are abundant. I've prepared a large platter of salad, which looks very colorful. I love playing with colors. It adds an extra dimension to food for me.

We engage in small talk to keep the conversation light. After the meal, as we relax on my bench and enjoy a cup of tea, I bring up the topic of bullying.

"Max," I say, "regarding bullying, I've done a lot of research and had many discussions with child psychologists. The conversations I had with them were invaluable. They gave me a better understanding of how bullying arises and what it entails. I used to think it was solely related to the victims' negative self-image. While that is a significant factor for most children, there's more to it.

"No two cases of bullying are exactly the same, but it always happens to people who are different from others. Children who are thin or overweight, tall or short, highly gifted or not as quick, with red hair, a different skin color, or a different culture, children with disabilities or illnesses, with a speech impediment or who speak very little, children who struggle to express their emotions. They can all become targets. Not all children who are different are bullied. It depends on how you react to comments. But if it happens to you, it may happen so subtly that you don't even realize it yourself. You receive confirmation for something you already believe about yourself. Both of us have experienced this, right, Max?"

"Yes," he nods, rubbing his leg—probably a bruise that's either painful or itchy.

"Max," I say, "I want to give you a few simple tips that can already make a difference. We'll go deeper into this later, but you don't have to wait to begin."

"First, stand tall. Lift your chest, roll your shoulders back, and hold your head high. Imagine there's an invisible thread gently pulling the crown of your head upward. Walk with confidence. Even if it feels strange at first, do it anyway. You're allowed to take up space."

"Now, your breath. When things get tense, we often stop breathing without realizing it. Or we breathe too fast. When that happens, place a hand on your belly. Breathe in slowly through your nose, then out through your mouth—longer than you breathed in. Do it a few times, calmly."

I pause for a moment.

"These may seem small," I say, "but they help more than you think. Later, I'll give you more—things you can say or do when something happens. But those only really work if you begin to see yourself differently. The way you think about who you are—that's where real change begins."

"For now, just begin with this: Standing tall. Breathing calmly. That's a good place to start."

We sit in silence for a moment.

Then I shift slightly. "The first question is: where does it come from: how we think about ourselves and what we believe? How did that self-image come about? I've talked about this before, but I want to delve deeper into it.

"We form an image of ourselves based on how people in our environment treat us. What do they say to us? What do we understand? What conclusions do we draw from it? How do they see the world, and what thoughts or belief systems do we adopt from them? That's how we form a self-image. Look at babies, how happy and carefree they are. The whole world revolves around them. But we gradually become aware of our surroundings and we change the truth about ourselves. We no longer see ourselves as the beautiful, perfect creatures we are, but we see ourselves through distorted lenses. And we create defense mechanisms to grow up and live in the safest possible world.

"How do we think about that world? Most people constantly live in a defensive posture. They are always alert to danger, to an attack on them. But that is an unhealthy way of living. They live with constant heightened stress and are always on guard. They are fixated on what is happening in the external world. Are you still following me, Max?"

"Yes, I understand."

"Increased stress hormone production," I continue, "is very natural in emergencies, when you need to flee immediately. It is very practical for your body to produce it to give you extra strength, but in everyday situations, it is unhealthy.

"Look at the animal kingdom. Everything is beautifully arranged there. When a lion hunts its prey, it starts running (increased stress hormone production). Once it has caught the prey (or not), it goes back to lounging, and the increased stress hormone production stops.

"If we constantly remain in a defensive stance, with elevated stress levels, we undermine our bodies. We make ourselves sick or suffer from burnout. Just look around at how many people live like that.

"Therefore, our thoughts are very important: how do we think about ourselves and the world? What goes through our minds?

"It is unfortunately natural to focus on the negative and constantly be on the lookout for problems. But you must realize that our thoughts are powerful instruments. With them, we create or break our own world. You should also know that *you* are in control of your own thoughts, even if no one has ever taught you that. Although, if you look at old writings, you will find this truth. 'As a man thinketh, so is he,' says the Bible. If you understand how your thoughts work, you can also change your thoughts.

"Say that you constantly tell yourself:

"*I am always alone.*

"They always pick on me.
"People cannot be trusted.
"The world is not a safe place to live.
"I am fat.
"I am stupid.
"I can't do this; I can't do that.

"You understand what I mean. Using these thoughts, you confine yourself in your own prison, and your mind, or consciousness, will faithfully provide countless examples to confirm what you think about yourself and the world. What you think becomes a truth for you. Your thoughts go on autopilot.

"To break free from this old pattern, you must change the thoughts and feelings about yourself and the world. We create our world and everything that happens in it. We are 100 percent responsible for what happens in our world."

Max looks at me blankly and incredulously. "I don't understand the last part. Can you explain it more simply?"

"OK, let me put it differently. What you think, you emit. It's like a radio tuned to a specific frequency. Someone else can pick up that signal. You are the transmitter, and the other person is the receiver. Let's say, for example, you're transmitting music on the 105.3 frequency, and someone else has tuned their radio to 105.3. They will hear the music you're broadcasting. The same is true of your thoughts. These are the natural laws of vibration and attraction, and they always work, without exceptions.

"Suppose you go to school and think beforehand: 'I hope nothing happens. I hope they don't pick on me. I hope nothing happens to my homework that I worked on until late last night. Should I put my new sweater in my schoolbag before entering the schoolyard or not?'

That doesn't help you feel better. First, you already feel nauseous before going to school. You arrive with a stomachache and are bullied before the first class even begins. You are sending this energy to school, and they pick it up. That's how you get what you expect."

Max turns red and angrily shouts at me, "Ridiculous! You and your fancy explanations and so-called natural laws! Are you saying that all of this is my own fault and that I ask for it—to be beaten up every day? That I do it to myself: my bruises, torn clothes, the humiliation? You're out of your mind. I don't want to hear another word. You won't see me again."

Furious, he storms off, half running down the path. Along the way to the gate, he kicks a large decorative stone on the side of my path. With a loud crash, he slams the garden gate shut. He leaves behind an intense silence.

I remember that someone once told me, "You are 100 percent responsible for what happens in your life," and, "What you send out, you receive back." I struggled to accept it then, and it took some time for me to come to terms with it.

How else could I have explained it to Max?

11

Anger

Max

Fuming, I run down the path. Ridiculous—what does she think? That I asked for all this bullying myself? That it's all my fault for what they do at school? You must be out of your mind to think that. Angrily, I kick a stone in my way, and with a searing pain in my foot, I continue running. I try to move forward as quickly as possible, away from this place. I thought she would help me, but I was mistaken.

With a slam, I shut the garden gate behind me. I start walking more slowly. I feel my right foot sticking in my sandal. When I look at my foot, to my great horror, I see that my toe is bleeding heavily. As if that's not enough! We can add that to the list.

What a day. My foot keeps bleeding more and more. The front of my sandal has turned completely red. And I have to go to school with that. If they see me like this, they'll have a good laugh, and I don't want to give them that satisfaction. How do I make myself invisible?

I need to find a solution. Maybe I should have just ended it back then. The opportunity was perfect. How long do I have to endure all of this? I still have a few years of school ahead.

I can't talk to my parents about it. I'm so ashamed that I'm the target of the class. A boy has to stand up for himself, be tough, handle his own problems. Why was I born into a family with only girls? My older sister doesn't understand me; I can't talk to her. She clearly comes from Venus. The only support I had is spouting nonsense about energy and how it's my fault that I'm being bullied, that I cause everything myself. But what if what she says is true? What if these natural laws exist?

12

Collapse

The next day, I wake up early. I toss and turn in my bed. It was a long night. I was afraid to go to sleep, and I had several nightmares again. I must have checked my phone at least twenty times to see if there was a message. Of course, I found a few edited photos of me again. I'm tired and frustrated, with a feeling of powerlessness and a sickening in my stomach. I feel nauseous. I rush out of bed and head to the bathroom. To top it off, the door is locked. I hear my sister singing loudly on the other side. I can't hold it in anymore and vomit all the food from yesterday. Ma, who just arrives, is livid. I feel really strange, a feeling I've never experienced before. It makes me anxious. It's as if I'm floating, and there's no ground beneath my feet. I hear voices, very distant, like an echo.

I regain consciousness in my bed. How did I end up here? What happened? I look at my clock and see that it's half past eleven. It's light outside. How is that possible? What day is it? Slowly, the memory of this morning comes back: feeling unwell in front of the bathroom door. But what happened after that?

How did I end up back in bed, so late on a Friday? Did I go back to bed by myself? How is that possible? Ma always makes sure everyone leaves on time. I don't understand. I want to get up and see if maybe someone is downstairs, but I feel so dizzy that I fall back onto the bed. I'll wait a little. It will probably pass. I've never experienced this before. It makes me anxious.

I'm thinking about yesterday afternoon. It was worse than usual—a complete catastrophe. First, I went to the nurse's office to clean my foot. Then I sneaked into the classroom as inconspicuously as possible, but they use that red disinfectant at school. It seeped through the bandage, so I became the target again. I was relieved when I was back home in the evening.

I think about the conversations with Helena. What should I do with all of this? I'm glad she told me about nutrition. I read through my notes to see what I've eaten in the past week. It's impressive. I started adding the calories next to them, which is really scary. If I eat two of my favorite cookies, that's already 700 calories! How many calories are you actually allowed to eat per day?

She gave me all kinds of other tips—some of them practical, others more about how I think and feel. Tips like walking tall, breathing deeply when I feel tense. I haven't tried those last two yet.

Where is my phone? It's always on my nightstand. Where did I put it? I decide to try getting up again. I walk unsteadily to the door. I hear Ma talking downstairs; she's probably on the phone. How is she already home? Normally she works until six o'clock. I hold onto the stair railing tightly as I slowly descend.

"Mom," I say. She turns around in the kitchen. "Max, are you OK? You scared me this morning. I called my work and took a day off."

"But Mom, you didn't have to do that. I'm old enough to stay home alone."

"Max, you should have seen yourself. You were pale as a ghost and didn't react to anything we said. I thought it was a good idea to stay home."

I feel guilty. She sacrificed a day off just for me. I take a seat at the kitchen table.

"Mom," I say, "I'm tired of being overweight. I want to eat more vegetables. I know you don't have time to cook elaborate meals in the evening. When you come home you're busy with the baby. Would you be willing to teach me how to cook, or tell me how to do it?"

"How sweet of you, but you don't have time either, with school and homework."

"Ma, how could we solve this?"

13

Putting It into Practice

It's been a few days, and I'm finally starting to feel a bit better. I've slept for hours and feel the urge to get some fresh air. There's a park nearby that I can go to. I drag myself over there. It's awful being this overweight—everything wobbles, and I'm out of breath after just a few steps.

It's three in the afternoon, and I'm sure I won't run into anyone. Near the entrance is a small lake, and I decide to sit down in the grass by the water. I want to reflect on everything that's been happening and on what Helena said. My head is a mess. I remember her advice: when you're stressed, focus on your breathing. I try to concentrate on my breath, and little by little, I start to feel calm.

Suddenly, I notice the birds in the trees nearby, singing beautifully. A frog croaks close to me, and soon others join in. They're so loud they almost drown out the birds. How am I supposed to concentrate with all this noise? I continue walking through the park and stop at the first bench I see, gratefully sinking into it. I still feel weak after the collapse.

After all those conversations with Helena, I realize I've learned a lot. But learning is one thing—doing something with it is another. I need to find a way to apply what she's told me.

I open my notebook and go through everything I've written down: nutrition, posture, thinking differently, visualizing, observing my thoughts, and more. It's a lot. But I remember what she said about taking small steps. You don't have to do everything at once—just something to get started.

Let's start with nutrition—how I fuel my body. But also the connection with the way I think about my body, how I perceive myself, and whether I can accept myself the way I am now. Helena said that acceptance doesn't mean staying stuck. It just means being honest about what is, recognizing that my past thoughts and habits created this body. She gave me a sentence: "Today I am creating new habits and thoughts for my future." Hmm. I need to work on that.

My weight: be clear. How many kilos do I want to lose? What's a healthy weight for a boy my age and height? Luckily, I have my phone with me to look it up.

I go to the website of the World Health Organization (WHO), which Helena once mentioned as a reliable source. I type in my age—fourteen years—and my height: 5 feet, five inches. Then I need to fill in my weight.

But how heavy am I really? I decide to stop by the pharmacy on my way home to weigh myself.

Then there's posture. Helena told me: "Stand tall. Lift your chest, roll your shoulders back, and hold your head high.

Imagine there's an invisible thread gently pulling the crown of your head upward."

Looking it up online, I read that posture plays a big role in how others see you. When you stand upright, you radiate confidence and authority. Slouching makes you seem uninterested and unsure of yourself. Roll your shoulders back, relax your upper body, but keep your core engaged. Walk with confidence. Even if it feels strange at first, do it anyway. You're allowed to take up space. Confident people take longer strides and walk at a steady rhythm. Practicing with the beat of an upbeat song can help. And it's not just about the pace: place your feet under your shoulders, push your chest slightly forward, straighten your back, chin up. Look the world in the eye and smile.

Research has shown that posture affects how we feel about ourselves. One helpful technique I found is something called "power posing"—standing tall with your arms and legs slightly spread. It's supposed to reduce cortisol (the stress hormone) and increase testosterone, which helps boost confidence. It's not something you do in front of others, more like a private way to energize yourself and boost your mindset before stepping into something that requires courage.

Confident walking also creates a great first impression. Without saying a word, your body tells others: *I'm here. I matter.* It's easy to fall back into old habits like slouching or staring at the ground when you feel uncomfortable, but that just makes you look scared. And I don't want to look scared anymore.

I slowly walk home and stop by the pharmacy. There's a long line, and I almost don't have the courage to wait. When it's finally my turn, I ask in a tiny voice if they have a scale I can use. The woman behind the counter didn't quite hear me and repeats loudly, "You want to weigh yourself?" I nod. I've already forgotten my plan to speak up clearly.

I step on the scale and see the number: 231 pounds. The woman raises her eyebrows in concern. I thank her quickly and rush out of the pharmacy. I don't want questions or comments.

Back home, I open my laptop and return to the WHO website. I find a body mass index percentile chart and use an online calculator.

When I fill in my current weight—231 pounds—the result says I'm in the obese range. *Obese.* That word hits me like a slap in the face.

The healthy range for someone my age and height is between 114 and 149 pounds, it says. Overweight starts at around 150 pounds, and obesity is about 174 pounds and up.

I quickly close the tab and stare at the wall. I knew I had gained weight, but I didn't think it was that bad. Still, something inside me refuses to spiral into shame. Not this time.

I think of what Helena said: Don't judge yourself. Observe. Learn. Adjust. Be kind to yourself. So I breathe. Deep in, long out. This is where I am now. But it doesn't have to be where I stay.

I look at the clock. I have half an hour before my sister gets home. She has a big mirror in her room, one where I can see my full body. Perfect to try out a power pose and check how I really stand. I also read once that if you want to walk straighter, try balancing a book on your head.

I quietly sneak into her room. Where is the mirror? There it is, in the corner, partly covered with a curtain. I stand in front of it and barely dare to look. What a terrible body! I hear Helena's voice in my ear: "Be kind to yourself." OK. No criticism. I'm working toward having and keeping a healthy, slim body.

It's been a long time since I looked at myself from head to toe. I grab an old book from her shelf, something she won't miss, and place it carefully on my head. Just then, the door swings open.

My sister stares at me. "What are you doing in my room, Max? And what's with the book on your head?"

There's no way out. I have to tell her the truth. "Well . . . I . . . I want to work on my confidence by walking more upright." I don't tell her about the bullying.

To my surprise, she doesn't laugh or make a snide comment. Instead, she says, "Do you want me to help you?"

I nearly faint. I've never heard her say that. Usually we're fighting, or she ignores me completely. I blush. "Yes, if that's OK."

She nods. "The book you chose is too small—it'll slide off too easily. Here, use the one I used."

You did this too?" I ask in surprise.

Yeah, about a year ago I worked on my posture. Right now, just balance it on your head. Don't walk yet. Find your balance first."

"OK, sounds good. If I can do that, I'll ask you for more tips."

She nods. I hesitate, then go for it. "I also read about something called a power pose—standing tall with arms and legs slightly spread. It's supposed to boost your confidence."

Celine smiles. "That's a really good one. I use it too. And you know what? There's another version that helps me a lot."

She pauses and then says, "Remember that movie with Wonder Woman? The way she stands with her hands on her hips?"

Oh yeah, I remember."

"Well, that's one version of a power pose. It gives you energy, makes you feel strong. It's something you do for yourself, like a secret boost. Great for when you need to pep yourself up before something important."

"OK, that's clear. Thanks, Celine. It's really great that you want to help me."

She smiles.

I turn around and head to my own room, book in hand.

14

Apologies

Helena

Two months have passed. I've been super busy with my work, but from time to time, my thoughts go to Max. I haven't received any signs of life from him. I wonder how he's doing.

It's a warm late summer day. I'm walking in my beloved forest, just a few steps away from my house. It helps me quiet my thoughts and be present in the here and now. I make it a habit to take twenty minutes for a walk. I often spend the whole day behind the computer, and that's not really healthy for my body. A body needs movement; otherwise, our muscles will become weak.

I inhale the delightful forest air. Suddenly I see a deer in front of me on the forest path. I know there are some families around here. It seems they even walk the streets very early in the morning with their little ones during springtime. I clearly surprise it, and with big leaps it runs off the path and disappears among the trees. In fact, I'm just as surprised as the deer.

I happily continue my way. When I arrive home, I make myself a cup of tea and decide to sit under the big tree. As I walk towards my bench, I notice colored paper lying there. That's strange. As I get closer, I see a bouquet of flowers. Who could they be from? Is there a card? I stand there in awe, looking at the beautiful flowers, when I hear a sound behind me. I turn around and see Max standing there.

"Max. Hi!" I'm not sure what else to say. He looks good. I have the impression that he has lost some weight, but it could be my imagination. There's something different about him—he stands straighter, more present.

"Do you like them?" he asks.

"Oh, did you put them there? How sweet! Yes, they're beautiful. I love mixed-color bouquets. How are you?" I ask. "I'm sorry I made you so angry last time. I didn't choose my words carefully enough."

"I actually came here today to apologize," says Max. "It wasn't nice what I said to you."

"Apology accepted."

I can see that Max is relieved. It had really bothered him.

"But how did you know I would come to the tree quickly?" I continue.

"Very simple. I know that when you have your walking shoes on and enter the forest, you usually stay away for about half an hour."

"So you've been spying on me?"

"Yes, twice. I wanted to apologize, but I didn't have the courage. Then I thought flowers might help. I know you love nature."

"You're observant," I say with a smile. We both burst into laughter, and the ice is broken.

"Would you like something to drink, Max?"

"Yes, a glass of water, please."

I look at him with a smile. Apparently he has learned quite a lot.

Max is the first to speak up. "How did you end up researching bullying? I know you were bullied in the past, but to do research on it?"

"That wasn't initially the reason. I'm a coach, and in the Netherlands, I used to give courses to adults dealing with low self-esteem and self-image. Confidence and a healthy sense of self-worth are the two most important things for me to move forward in life. I wanted to pass on my knowledge to children, to teach them at a young age how to take charge of their own lives. I wanted to show them the power of their thoughts and how they can learn to face life with confidence. I searched and researched what was available on the market. A few years ago, I finally found the solution. I decided to write a book about bullying in schools."

"And?" Max asks.

"It was very interesting to conduct the research, and I learned a lot from it. I had some fascinating discussions with psychologists about how bullying arises and why it exists. I discovered that group dynamics play a significant role in this phenomenon. I wanted to understand what goes on in the mind of a bully, why they do what they do. Of course, you can't generalize about all cases, and each situation is unique, but there are some common threads.

"While writing my book, I realized—and this may sound strange—that I myself had experienced bullying. I now understood why the psychologists kept saying: it happens to the victim without their awareness, because what the bully says feels like the truth to them. It was a shock to see what had happened in my own life. I had isolated myself during my school years, trying to blend in as inconspicuously as possible so they would leave me alone. Of course, I didn't entirely succeed.

"Looking back on that period, I now know that I am 100 percent responsible for what happens in my world. Whether consciously or unconsciously, I attract certain situations. Of course, back then, I didn't consciously ask for it; no one does. It's an unconscious pattern that exists within us. I've already told you: we pick up thoughts from the world around us and believe in them, both consciously and unconsciously."

15

Why Bullying Occurs

I walk over to my desk and retrieve a document.

"Look, Max, this is the report* that summarizes my research findings. It's a copy, so you can take it home and read it at your own pace.

"In broad terms, it states that bullying is prohibited by law. There are international rights for children that protect them, ensuring a safe upbringing.

"There's one thing you mustn't forget: *it's not your fault that you're being bullied.* The foundation of bullying is fear. It's about exerting power over another person by making them afraid. In every instance of bullying, three elements are present: Bullying occurs repeatedly against the same person. There is an imbalance (in power, strength, or social status), and bullying is intentional. There are different forms of bullying: verbal, physical, material, relational, digital, or sexual.

"It can begin as early as four or five years old. At that age,

---

* *(To the reader: you can find this complete report in the appendix of this book.)*

bullying is different compared to when one is older. It's less calculated and more about who is the strongest. With teenagers, bullying becomes more conscious, perverse, and cruel. In girls, bullying tends to happen very subtly: a glance, a word, an attitude. In boys, it manifests more as physical violence. It's possible for a teenager to accept humiliation to fit in with the group. This is often seen among girls. Or they may be afraid to assert their boundaries within the group because of shame or fear of not being accepted.

"A group always consists of leaders and followers. A leader wants to be in charge. If you side with the bully in the group, you know that you won't be the target. The followers are safe. If children have to choose between the bully and the victim, they choose the bully.

"The basis is that the victim is somehow different from the other children, such as being tall, short, overweight, thin, shy, introverted, or overly serious, or having a different skin color. They are vulnerable. They have a negative self-image and lack belief in themselves. Deep down, they are fearful, and the bully exacerbates this fear. It happens to children who, in addition to the aforementioned characteristics, may live in a fantasy world or be highly gifted or distant.

"A child who is being bullied may exhibit various symptoms. It may manifest as rebellious behavior, a consistently bad mood, being defiant, leading to frequent conflicts at home or school. They may refuse to go to school or study, experience headaches or stomachaches before leaving home. Suddenly their grades drop, or they struggle with concentration issues. They come home with scratches, bruises, torn clothing, a missing backpack or schoolbag.

"Or they become quiet, lose interest in playing, isolate themselves. They have few or no friends. They may gain or lose a significant amount of weight or lose their appetite. They experience sleep problems or may suddenly start bedwetting. Some may even attempt suicide.

"It's important for the victim to work on what we're doing here together. Consider these possibilities: learning to say no, understanding your emotions, not automatically becoming angry, stepping out of the victim role, understanding your values, knowing yourself, loving and respecting yourself. Live in the present moment and achieve successes to build your self-confidence.

"Another finding from my research is that children who act as class clowns are not usually bullied, even though they are different. Attitude is also crucial, as is self-confidence. You can improve self-confidence by participating in judo or another sport. Girls benefit greatly from dancing or sports. Fencing is the best option; it helps command respect and establish personal boundaries.

"It helps a child to defend themselves with nonaggressive words: never respond to the bully with the same aggression. Look for a humorous response. Practice your responses at home with a sibling or a good friend so that you come across confidently when you reply to the bully. You only get one chance to say it."

16

Visualization and Connecting with Your Desires

"Wow, that's quite something that came up in your research," says Max, looking up from the document.

"Yes, it really opened my eyes. It's what I told you before. I thought it was only related to a negative self-image, but there's more to it."

"But what can I do to get out of this situation?" Max asks.

"There's only one thing you can do: work on yourself. You can't change the external world, but you can change your inner world. Your life is the result of how you perceive and experience the world. Two things are important: how do you nourish your mind (your thoughts) and how do you nourish your body? Because that nourishment affects your mind as well.

"Let's focus on thoughts: What do you think? What thoughts constantly occupy your mind? What does that little voice in your head say? Are they fearful thoughts, or thoughts of hope and trust? What you emit, you attract. If you are fearful, you emit fearful thoughts and feelings, which in turn attract fearful situations. It's like a boomerang. It always comes back, just as the energy you emit comes back to you, giving you more of what you emit.

"It's quite simple, once you understand the system. The same goes for your body. If you eat unhealthy food, you can't expect to have a healthy body, and unhealthy nourishment also affects your mind. Remember what I told you about sugar? The same applies to your thoughts: if you have negative or fearful thoughts, you can't expect to feel happy and joyful. You need to align your thoughts with what you want to achieve.

"What kind of life do you want for yourself? You are the only one who decides how you want to live: it's your life. Do you want to feel happy, cheerful, relaxed, or unhappy and sad? You can let the outside world influence you. You can wonder, 'What do they think of me? Am I good enough in their eyes or not?' You can also let others determine what happens in your life, but then you're playing a supporting role in your own life, and someone else takes the lead. We see this in people who always want to please others.

"Of course, you're still a teenager, and you have parents or caregivers to deal with. But even now you can express your wishes and be open to their advice. That doesn't mean you have to adopt all their thoughts and feelings. You decide for yourself what you accept and what you don't. Even if you have an overly protective mother who sees danger in everything, you can still decide to have trust in life. You can choose which situations you want to engage in and which ones you don't, and decide not to be fearful of everything beforehand.

"Your body is always giving signals about how you feel and whether you're in harmony with your inner self, which knows what's best for you and always encourages you to be the best version of yourself. It strives to make you feel happy and joyful. When you're not in harmony with yourself, your body sends out signals: first weak signals, and then stronger ones. You experience them as low energy, headaches, skin problems, physical discomfort, broken limbs, organ dysfunction, illnesses. Ignoring these signals can even lead to death."

"Isn't that going a bit too far?" Max asks.

"It sounds intense," I reply, "but sometimes we're not aware of what we constantly say or think. If someone constantly says, 'That will be the death of me,' look at how old they are when they die and under what circumstances. It can also be a slow death.

"Let me give you an example of the power of thoughts. I once read about a man who was on the run and hid in a refrigerated train car. When they found him dead in the wagon, he exhibited all the symptoms of hypothermia. It turned out that the cooling system wasn't even turned on. He was so convinced that he would freeze to death that it actually happened.

"Another example is the story of a woman who lived in a big house and kept saying, 'I hate this house. It's way too big. I wish I lived in a small shack.' Several years later, her husband passed away, leaving her with huge debts. The house and all her possessions had to be sold, and she ended up living in a small shack.

"You see, you have to be careful with what you constantly tell yourself, whether aloud or in your thoughts. Even if you repeatedly say something negative as a joke, the universe doesn't understand it as a joke and takes it as truth, giving you more of what you ask for.

"The positive side, of course, is that we can create what we want. We have to truly want it, believe in it, and feel it. We imagine already having what we want. We visualize it as vividly as possible, hearing what we want to hear, smelling, tasting, and feeling it, and never doubting it. It becomes a new truth for you.

"Let me give you another metaphor. You're in a restaurant, studying the menu: what would you like to eat; what brings you joy? Then you decide, it's chicken with freshly steamed seasonal vegetables. You place your order with the waiter and wait for him to serve you the delicious meal. In your mind, you already see the plate being placed in front of you. You admire the beautiful colors on your plate. You smell a delightful aroma rising, and the thought of eating all that goodness even makes your mouth water. You taste it, savoring the food, letting the warm mixture move around in your mouth. You hear the gentle grinding of your teeth as they chew the food.

"This is essentially the whole process. You decide what you want. You ask for it and expect it to come. Imagine that after you've placed your food order, you start doubting. After five minutes you call the waiter over to your table and ask, 'Are you sure they're preparing my order in the kitchen?' A few minutes later, you stop him again and say, 'You're really sure they're making it, right?' Then you ask him again. Next time you won't even be allowed in the restaurant. By doubting like that, you're saying, 'I asked for it, but I don't believe in it.'

"It's not 'seeing is believing,' but the opposite: 'believing is seeing.' The universe always says, 'I'll give you more of what you want.'

"Doubt is the dominant energy of 'not having.' When you say, 'I don't have,' the universe says, 'OK, I'll give you more of "not having."'

"When you have a hunch, something that comes from within, you have to act on it. You can't just sit on a chair and wait for it to come because that's not how it works. Often, the things you desire come to you in surprising ways, in ways you couldn't have imagined in a million years. That's the beauty of the universe. *You ask, the universe gives, and you have to be open to receiving it.*"

"I don't fully understand," says Max. "What do you mean by saying, 'When you have a hunch, you have to act on it'?"

"Hunches are thoughts that come to you without your knowing why. For example, you're supposed to go to the supermarket, and something tells you, 'Go an hour later.' When you get to the supermarket, you bump into the exact person you needed because he builds houses, and you're looking for a house.

"A hunch can take the form of an interview you hear on the radio or TV, or something you read in a book. It can be a conversation between two people. But you immediately know that it's information, a message for you. You feel it. It's important that you respond to those hunches by taking action. Do you understand what I mean?"

"Yes, it's clear to me now," Max replies.

"By the way, how is your nutrition going, Max? Have you found a solution for that?"

"Yes, I talked to my mom. We decided that we'll go grocery shopping together once a week, on Friday evenings, so it takes her less time to read all those labels. What's really cool is that she's teaching me how to cook. We bought a simple cookbook with some explanations about nutrition in the beginning. And I have to be honest: cooking is something I really enjoy. Especially when everyone is enjoying the food and complimenting me. Sometimes they don't say it, but I can see on their faces that they're enjoying it, and that makes me very happy."

"That's fantastic, Max. I have the impression that you've already lost some weight; is that correct?"

"Yes, I'm very proud of that. I've already lost twenty pounds."

"Wow, congratulations. You've done really very well."

"Thank you. It motivates me to keep going," says Max with a big smile on his face.

"Amazing. So you've found a rhythm in that?"

"Absolutely. And my mom has lost ten pounds, which she's very happy about, because she couldn't lose it before. Now she wants to lose another twenty pounds. Now we're motivated together."

I laugh.

"That's the ripple effect. You start with a baby step, and in a short time it has significant consequences for yourself and others."

"I'm super happy about it," says Max. "That's why I feel so guilty for being so mean to you."

"I completely understand your reaction. It took me a while too before I was willing to accept that I'm 100 percent responsible for my own life. By the way, Max, don't blindly believe everything I tell you, but remain critical and believe in what you want. Do your own research on what feels right for you. Everyone has their own values and belief system. It's good to observe that in yourself and see if your beliefs support or hinder you.

"With the universal laws, on the other hand, you can choose to believe in them or not, but they always work, because that's how it is with a law. We just talked about 'what you emit, you attract.' That's the law of vibration, the main law; the law of attraction is a corollary. But I won't overwhelm you with all those laws. If you find it interesting, delve into them a bit more."

"And now?" Max asks.

"There are many things you can do to work on yourself, but you've already taken the first step, balancing your eating habits, and it's going great. If I understand correctly, you've found your groove with that. And I see your posture and energy have shifted too."

Max looks down for a moment, then meets my eyes. "Yeah. That started after I stormed off that day. I was so angry—I didn't want to hear anything anymore."

I nod slowly, giving him space.

"The next day, I crashed completely. Couldn't get out of bed. I felt like I was drowning." He pauses. "But a few days later, I took out my notes. The ones from our talks. I read about posture, about walking tall. That same afternoon, when I was home alone, I sneaked into my sister's room. She has a big mirror."

A faint smile touches his lips.

"I was trying to stand up straight and walk tall like you told me about . . . and balancing a book on my head. And then of course she walked in."

I smile softly. "Oh no . . ."

"I thought she'd laugh. I was ready to feel humiliated all over again. But she didn't. She just looked at me and asked what I was doing. When I told her, she didn't mock me. She offered to help."

Max shakes his head in quiet disbelief. "She even showed me how she had practiced the same thing, a year ago. That moment—it changed something, I think in both of us."

"Sometimes the smallest moment opens a door. I'm so glad you walked through it."

I pause for a moment, then continue, making sure my voice is warm and steady.

"Now let's start with the vision of how you want your life to be. I already told you that what you emit, you attract. So, it's important to know what you want to attract and what you no longer want to attract."

"That seems quite clear to me. I want the bullying to stop. I want to be left alone."

"Yes, so what's important is your perception of the whole situation. Right now, you only see the aggression, the attacks on you; is that correct?"

"Yes, that's correct. I already worry in the morning about what will happen throughout the day. They target me every day, so what will it be today?"

"OK. Those are your thoughts. Now we need to transform those thoughts into something you want. Close your eyes for a few minutes and imagine the life you desire. How do you see yourself and your surroundings? Relax and let your imagination run wild."

"I find it very difficult to imagine that," says Max.

"OK, let's do the visualization together then."

"What's visualization?"

"Forming a mental image of what you want. I'll guide you into a very relaxed state. Another word for it is *hypnosis*. Rest assured, it's completely safe. You are and always remain in control of what happens. The worst that can happen is that you fall asleep. It has happened to me a few times. I recorded a visualization on my phone, and I became so relaxed by my own voice that I talked myself to sleep. I didn't hear at least half of it and only woke up towards the end. I was wonderfully relaxed, but that wasn't the purpose of the exercise."

We both laugh.

"Let's begin," I say. "Place your feet comfortably on the ground and connect with the earth. Relax completely. Close your eyes. Breathe in through your nose for a count of four. Hold it for three counts. And exhale through your mouth for a count of five. Repeat this several times until you feel calm and relaxed. Let go of all your thoughts. Focus solely on your breathing. Good. Continue with your breaths. You feel relaxed. I'll count down from 10 to 0, and you'll feel more and more relaxed: 10, 9, 8, relax even more; 7, 6, 5, you feel more and more relaxed; 4, 3, 2, relax even more; 1, 0, you are completely relaxed. You feel good, you are safe."

Slowly, with a gentle voice, I continue: "You find yourself in a beautiful forest. Look around. What do you see? Is it a dense forest or an open forest? Are the trees thin or thick? Are they tall? What else do you see? Do you see animals walking or in the trees? What sounds do you hear? Do you hear birds singing or other animal sounds? What do you smell? Do you smell the morning dew, or the moss, or the trees? Do you smell something else? Immerse yourself completely in your surroundings; observe all the details. You feel fantastic, and you feel the soft moss beneath your feet. Next to you, you hear a stream babbling, and you follow it. You enjoy being here. You feel joyful, relaxed, and free.

"In the distance, you see a bridge. You walk towards it, all the while enjoying the surroundings. As you reach the bridge, you see the city on the other side of the water. You walk across the long bridge, and you hear the sounds of the city. You enter the city. You feel happy. It's a very special day. Look around. What do you notice? As you arrive in the city center, you see a lot of friends standing there. They have smiles on their faces; they're delighted to see you. How do they greet you? What words do they use? And how do you feel?

"They have something important to give you. It's a box wrapped in beautiful paper. Slowly you unwrap it. What could be inside? What are they surprising you with? You open the box and look at what's inside with joy. It's so beautiful, so thoughtful, that tears of emotion well up in your eyes. You take the gift and thank everyone warmly. Then you walk back to the bridge with the treasure in your hands, feeling so appreciated. You take a little jump of happiness. You follow the stream back to the point where you started your walk, enjoying your surroundings.

"This is the moment to return. I'll count from 0 to 10, and when I reach 10, you'll be wide awake: 0, 1, 2, you feel relaxed and slowly come back; 3, 4, 5, you feel yourself becoming more awake; 6, 7, 8, you become more and more awake; 9, 10, you are wide awake and full of energy."

Slowly Max emerges from his visualization. He has a relaxed face and stretches. I give him a moment to recover and ask, "What did they give you, Max?"

"A key, a golden key. They said, 'This is the key to your happiness.'"

"How fantastic, Max. How does it feel?"

"I feel moved to receive such a beautiful gift."

"Yes," I say softly. "It is indeed a beautiful gift you have received. Now you know what affirmation you can use. What could you say to yourself?"

"I have the key to my own happiness. I open the doors to my happiness."

"That's beautiful."

"Visualization is so amazing! I never knew what it was," Max says.

"It is very powerful, and it gives you insights, or you receive a message that guides you about what to do. It connects you with your subconscious mind. Deep inside, you know exactly what you need and what brings you joy. Work with the affirmation and play with it, but also think about what makes you happy. Is it walking in the city or in a forest? Is it running, walking, dancing, or jumping? Make a list of what brings you joy, and do more of those things. We are born to be happy, and when we focus on that, we will attract more moments of joy."

"Thank you, Helena, that's great. I'll work on it."

17

Big News

Ten days later, the phone rings. It's Max. He asks if I have time today or tomorrow for him to come over. He has big news. We agree to meet the next afternoon. I have a canceled appointment, so it works out perfectly. The universe has once again arranged things beautifully.

The following day, as I am busy pruning my rose garden, Max cheerfully pushes open the garden gate. I hear him whistling a tune. It's another beautiful day, a breath of fresh air after a whole week of rain, which was actually beneficial for my garden, which needed a lot of water.

The climate has changed a lot here in the past few years. We hardly have distinct seasons anymore, and winter is very short. Every day, I am grateful to live and dwell in this beautiful place. I adore being in my garden. A part of it is my rose garden, and there is also a permaculture section where all my vegetables grow together. It's the easiest way to garden. Some people call it gardening for lazy folks. For me, it's the perfect approach, since I have limited time. This way, I can still enjoy delicious organic vegetables, and as a bonus, everything grows abundantly. The garden yields larger potatoes than I have ever seen before. Additionally, I have fruit trees: cherry, apple, Mirabelle plum, pear, chestnut, and a couple of walnut trees.

"Helena," Max calls out. "Are you in the garden?"

"I'm here, in the rose garden. I'm almost done pruning. Give me two more minutes."

Max approaches, still whistling, clearly enjoying the beautiful colors.

"Your roses are stunning, and I don't know which one it is, but there's one that smells really nice."

"That's the one you're standing close to."

Five minutes later, I finish up and tidy my tools. We head inside and settle ourselves on the comfortable couch in my living room. After a few minutes of small talk, I ask, "What's your big news? I'm so curious."

"Your visualization exercise has helped me tremendously, and I've started writing things down. I decided that I want to fulfill my deepest desire."

"What is that, Max? You're really piquing my curiosity now."

"I absolutely love piano music, and I want to be able to play the instrument perfectly."

"What a great idea! Music is definitely relaxing."

"There's just one obstacle," Max says. "Mom and Dad don't have the money for it. So I've decided to take on a paper route. With the money I earn, I can pay for my piano lessons."

"Max, that's a fantastic idea. Will you be walking or doing your route on a bike?"

"I've asked for a cart, so I can do it on foot, and I'm lucky, because the route is not far from my house. The papers are delivered to my doorstep every morning."

"Well, that's hitting three birds with one stone," I say enthusiastically. "First, you'll be walking more, which is good for your body. Second, you'll be earning your own money. And third, you'll be able to pay for your piano lessons."

"Yes, I'm really happy about it. I actually started my paper route last week."

"I can see you're not wasting any time," I wink at him.

Max gives me a teasing look. "Was it you who told me to strike while the iron is hot?"

I burst into laughter. "That might very well have been me."

"But it's just like you said, Helena. You have to know what you want first, and then the solution comes to you."

"You're a quick learner," I continue, laughing. "You grasp things quickly and put them into action. Let's celebrate your second victory. I want to give you a gift. I think it's the best gift I can give you: your first piano lesson."

"Oh, how incredibly kind of you. Thank you so much!" he exclaims, throwing his arms around me. He startles himself with his own spontaneity, and we both burst into laughter. Then he says, "Yes, that's just the thing that would make me the happiest. And Helena, may I ask you, how did you handle the bullying at school back then?"

18

Mirror Exercise

We interrupt our conversation to make some drinks in the kitchen. All this talking makes you thirsty. We take a seat at the solid wooden breakfast bar, which is invitingly adorned with comfortable black leather barstools. Then we continue our conversation.

"Going back to your question," I say, "in fact, when I was in school, I didn't recognize it as bullying. I just felt unhappy, and that was it. Now I know that I was being bullied by the way I saw myself, how I thought about myself, the words I said to myself, and how I carried myself. And that was reflected back to me by the outside world. The outside world is always like a mirror for us.

"Speaking of mirrors, that was one of the first exercises I learned on my personal development journey. It is incredibly valuable and confronting. I highly recommend it. It completely changed my life. That exercise taught me to love myself, to support and be kind to myself—to believe in myself, my own qualities, abilities, and unique talents. For me, it is one of the most important tools to develop a healthy self-image and be self-assured. As a result, I don't depend any more on the outside world to feel good and happy, no matter what other people say to me, what they think I can or cannot do, or whether I am suitable for something or not. Because if I seek approval from the outside world, it becomes a lifelong quest, and I will never find the solution.

"You see that with many people. They go through life like sheep, doing what others want them to do, or what they think others want them to do. Those people are often frustrated but don't stand up for themselves. To avoid thinking and feeling the pain, they seek solace in excessive drinking, smoking, or hours of mindless TV or scrolling through social media.

"If they were content with themselves, they wouldn't depend on whatever happens in the outside world. If they decided how their lives should be, they would take care of their own happiness, respect themselves, and receive respect from others because they have clearly set their boundaries.

"In the beginning, I used the mirror exercise to love myself unconditionally and look into my own eyes without any judgment. The first few weeks were very difficult. When I looked into my eyes and said to myself, 'I love you, I really love you,' I would burst into tears. So I had to make it lighter for myself, and I said, 'Helena, every day I love you more and more.'

"At first I didn't believe it at all. In the past, I had never listened to myself, so why would I suddenly believe that I could love myself, support myself, and appreciate myself? But that was just the old programmed voice in my head. To accept it, I had to soften it even more and said, 'I, Helena, am loving because I love animals. The same love I feel for them, I now give to myself.'

"After the initial flood of tears—because it was so overwhelming to want to give this love to myself—I persisted. I said it at least once every day, but especially in the beginning, I would say it three times a day.

"Little by little, I started to believe it, and I felt a warm feeling inside. Then I took it a step further and started using the 'you' form: 'Helena, you love yourself,' and then the 'she' form: 'Helena, she loves herself.'" The 'she' form represents the outside world and is also very powerful.

"I'm not sure exactly how long it took, but it was definitely several months before I truly started to believe it. Now when I pass by a mirror, for example, I say to myself, 'I love you, sweetheart,' or 'You're doing great,' or 'I'm proud of you,' or 'You're perfect just the way you are.' I say whatever spontaneously comes to my mind.

"You might ask, doesn't that make you conceited? No: love, attention, and encouragement for oneself are necessary, and they make you feel wonderful. Of course, it's still a great pleasure to receive a compliment from someone else, but I'm no longer dependent on it because I believe in myself. I know who I am, and I have confidence in myself.

"It is my duty to give myself unconditional love—to be my own best friend, to support and encourage myself, and to believe that I can rely on myself.

"Did you know that if you don't give love to a baby after birth, it dies? That's when you understand why love is so important.

"Let's be honest. How do we treat someone we love? We don't spend the whole day criticizing them. So don't do it to yourself either.

"I was the champion of self-criticism. It didn't get me anywhere; it only made me unhappy. This method of loving myself has given me peace. I no longer seek approval from my external world. I am relaxed. I'm no longer stressed because I always want to do everything perfectly. Even so, I still do my best, I give my best, and every day I become better and better at what I do.

"I look younger, I'm happy with my body, and I have radiant health. I feel comfortable in my own skin. I attract cheerful, positive, and loving people. I live in the house of my dreams, in a place I adore, and I have deep, loving, fulfilling relationships. I am a successful, internationally best-selling author, and I have sold millions of copies of my book. I do work that I love and make a positive impact on the lives of millions of people. I travel all over the world. In short, my life is one big celebration.

"But the mirror exercise alone is not enough. We also need to observe the voice in our head: what is it saying to us all day long?"

I glance at my watch and realize with a start that it's getting late. I ask Max, "Would you like to take a walk? I need to be at the post office by five o'clock."

"Sure," Max replies.

I put on my comfortable shoes, and we head towards the town.

19

What Energy Do You Emit?

It has become a habit for Max and me to see each other once or twice a week. I keep Wednesday afternoons free. That's the advantage of having your own business: you can manage your own time. The bond between Max and me has grown stronger, and he feels more liberated. I've had the privilege of enjoying his excellent cooking a few times as well. If music weren't his number one passion, he would undoubtedly make an excellent chef. He says he's inspired by my culinary skills. I'm glad I can contribute to his well-being.

Today we decide to sit outside on the terrace. It's a lovely spot, sheltered from the wind, and we're enjoying our cups of tea as usual.

"Max," I say, "often there are things I repeat because we learn through repetition. Sometimes I phrase it slightly differently, creating an aha! moment. A moment of recognition, understanding a concept through an alternative explanation.

"We've talked about affirmations. I want to emphasize that repetition is the key to change, but it's also crucial to feel in advance what it's like to achieve your goal. You may wonder why.

"Feeling is a vibration, an energy. We are all pure energy, and so is everything around us. We are connected to everything and everyone, but everyone emits their own frequency. When you're angry, you sent out a different frequency than when you're happy. As I mentioned before, like attracts like.

"For example, when I leave the house in the morning and give a smile to everyone I encounter, they all smile back. But when I'm stressed, no one smiles at me, and as a result of my low energy, I also attract unpleasant events. I get stuck in traffic, or people lash out at me. In concrete terms, something in you attracts bullying, or, rather, you unconsciously emit the energy that you are being bullied. The good news is that once you know and accept this, you can change your energy to attract what you do want.

"It is also important to detach how you think about yourself. If you think, 'I am a victim,' it becomes difficult to change yourself, because it has become a part of your identity. If you say, 'I have had a victim experience,' you detach it from your identity. Now you only need to change your experience into the one you desire.

"Of course, none of this happens automatically. It is not enough merely to be aware of this process. You must work on it daily. It took a long time to program yourself as you are today, so it is normal for it to take time to reprogram yourself. It is hard to say how long you will need to overwrite your old program: it depends on how long ago the original programming was installed and how deeply it is ingrained on your inner hard drive."

"OK, I understand that. But how is it possible that I am programmed this way and attract all this bullying?" Max asks, confused. "I didn't ask for this, did I?"

"No, of course you didn't consciously ask for it. It is subconscious. The way you unconsciously programmed yourself could have been influenced by someone in your environment who had low self-esteem, a negative self-image, or by someone who was overly anxious about your well-being, which gave you the unconscious impression that you couldn't stand up for yourself. These negative emotions send negative energy out into the world, and it is picked up by your subconscious. The unconsciously planted seeds in your subconscious that grew because you paid attention to them.

"It is not useful to know exactly where this messaging comes from. What's important is that to stop the bullying, you need to change the energy you emit in order to attract what you do want. If you start asking yourself questions like, 'Why am I being bullied? Why do I attract all this negativity? Why am I the target of the class?' you will only receive more of what you no longer want. The universe is very generous and gives you exactly what you ask for, even if you don't want it. In other words, you attract more of what you don't want.

"I challenge you to have a very clear image of what you *do* want. How do you want to see yourself? Do you want to communicate easily, be successful in certain areas? How do you want to feel? Do you want to be loved, accepted? Do you want joy and harmony?

"My first question to you now is, do you accept that you emit this energy yourself, and are you willing to change it?"

"Accepting is still a bit difficult for me," Max says, "but I am absolutely willing to change."

"I understand," I say, "but acceptance is a crucial key in this whole process. Otherwise, it is impossible to change yourself, because you will keep looking for excuses in the outside world. You'll be thinking, 'I haven't done anything, yet they keep targeting me at school.' Do you understand? You remain in the victim role. Nothing will happen without 100 percent acceptance that you are 100 percent responsible. But remember: You are only 100 percent responsible for the energy you emit and the events you attract. You are not responsible for someone else's actions: they are 100 percent responsible for their own actions."

"Ah," Max says, "I'm starting to understand better. But if I am 100 percent responsible and bully is too, doesn't that make it 200 percent when the total can only be 100 percent?"

"You're right. It simply means that each person is fully responsible for their own actions, not a portion of them. Let me be clear that it is absolutely not about getting angry at yourself for what happens to you or what has happened to you. Be careful not to feel guilty, because we tend to feel guilty quickly when we take 100 percent responsibility. I know all about it. But we don't gain anything by being angry with ourselves. So assuming that you fully accept that you emit that energy and want to change it, on a scale of 1 to 10, with 10 representing complete dedication, what score would you give your commitment?"

"Well," Max replies, "I get the impression that it won't be easy, but I am 100 percent willing to tackle it."

"OK, so a 10?"

"Yes, a 10 plus."

We both burst into laughter. He definitely has a sense of humor, I think. You need that when you're dealing with something as significant as self-worth and self-image, because, in essence, they are at the core of everything.

20

What Story Do You Tell Yourself?

"Max, today I want to explain an exercise to you that has given me a lot of insight into what I do and don't want. Let me be clearer about that.

"If I understand correctly, Max—and correct me if I'm wrong—you already make yourself nervous before going to school. Your desire to go drops below freezing point. In your mind, you can already see them waiting for you. You hear the jeers and the hurtful remarks. You feel them getting to you, pulling at you, or attacking you. You can already see it playing out like a movie, and you say to yourself, 'This is undoubtedly going to be another nightmare day.' You may even have a knot in your stomach, get a headache, or feel sick or anxious. That's what you do every day before going to school: you emit thoughts and feelings."

"Yes," Max says softly, realizing what he's been doing. "And what happens on that day?" I continue.

"They're waiting for me, and they don't miss a moment to make my life miserable," Max replies.

"In other words, it's another nightmare day?" I ask.

"Yes," Max says, tears welling up in his eyes.

"I understand that it's painful to think about, Max, but it's important that you make the connection between what you think—the energy you emit—and what happens. You're expecting what will happen that day, and that's exactly what happens. These thoughts and the feelings associated with this situation have been created and linked by you. Once you know they're linked, you can also unlink them, because you've created them, consciously or unconsciously.

"*Thoughts are linked to feelings, and feelings are linked to actions*. For example, you have anxious thoughts. They lead to anxious feelings, which emit anxious energy. As a result, you behave anxiously, consciously or unconsciously, and attract anxious situations. Like energy attracts like.

"You try to make yourself as small or inconspicuous as possible when you're at school, or you avoid a situation. You told me that you no longer eat in the cafeteria. The consequence is that you isolate yourself even more from the group. And there will probably be more situations like that.

"It's important to start telling yourself a different story: a story that doesn't make you feel sick and miserable, but makes you happy and joyful. When I want to change my own story, I use a very powerful exercise myself. It goes like this:

"I find a place where I can work undisturbed, turn off my phone, and let the people around me know that I don't want to be disturbed for the time being. Then I take two sheets of paper. On the first one, I write out the current situation, as it is today, complete with all the details. In your case, you write in great detail how you feel before going to school, what your thoughts are, what your fears are, and what happens at school. Everything. Your feelings and thoughts. Even the hatred. Let it all out. There are no limits to the words you use.

"I always have tissues at hand to feel my sadness and let it be. When I've finished writing and I have nothing more to add, I take my second sheet of paper and write in the present tense how I want the situation to be. I describe it as fully as possible, with all the details and a lot of feelings of happiness. I let my imagination run wild. I create my ideal picture. I don't wonder how I can make this happen; I simply write down what I want (as long as it remains ethically responsible and loving). Do you understand?"

He nods in agreement.

"Then I take the first sheet and burn it outside in a special pan. At first, I did it in my kitchen, but it smelled for days afterward," I add with a laugh. "Be careful with fire. Let your parents know what you're doing; make sure it's safe. It would be a disaster if the fire department had to come. Another thing you can do is shred the paper completely and throw it in the trash bin outside. Don't put it in the indoor trash bin, because we want it out of the house.

"You might ask, does this help change a situation? Not in and of itself. It's symbolic, letting go of the situation. It creates an opening. You communicate to your mind what you do want.

"Then I take a few positive statements, what I've called affirmations (that is, confirmations) of my ideal situation, and I write them out ten times every day. I bought a special notebook that I only use for this purpose.

"I also repeat the affirmations in my mind as much as possible throughout the day. And I visualize the desired situation. I live it. I feel it. I hear the things I want to hear. I smell the scents I want to smell. I feel how happy I am, and I immerse myself completely in a feeling of joy from having what I want. In the beginning, when I work with a new affirmation, sometimes I even set an alarm during the day to remind me to say it.

"To give you an example, before I got my house, I wrote down in great detail how I wanted it to be: the location, the number of rooms, how I wanted the kitchen to be, and why. After that, I constantly lived in my thoughts about that house. I enjoyed the morning sun on my skin in the kitchen as I had my breakfast. I smelled the aroma of freshly brewed coffee. I did my workouts in my gym and heard the birds singing through the open sliding doors. I saw the sparkling water of my swimming pool, inviting me to take a plunge. Then I enjoyed my beautiful desk and imagined myself happily writing books and creating programs. By noon, I heard sounds coming from the kitchen, and my nose was repeatedly delighted by the delicious cooking aromas, making me hungry. Or I pictured myself cooking with my loved ones and friends, having the best time and laughing together. I heard their contagious laughter and felt my belly shake from laughing so hard.

"You can do the same with friendships. Imagine how your ideal day at school would look like. For instance, visualize your classmates eagerly waiting for you at the entrance or on the schoolyard, happy to see you again. They appreciate your warm friendship, your honesty, your knowledge, and your kind and uplifting words. They value your opinion. Feel loved and fully accepted for who you are. Imagine them giving you an invitation to a party they are planning soon, and you can almost hear them begging you to come.

"Then see yourself attending the party. They are thrilled that you came and could make time for it. You are the center of attention. Imagine how much fun you have, hear their warm laughter when you say something funny. Notice their disappointment when you announce that you have to leave, and hear their attempts to persuade you to stay a little longer. Feel happy to have so many lovely people around you.

"See them sending you sweet messages on social media, thanking you for coming. Thanks to you, the party was a huge success.

"Of course, it might feel very surreal at first. You are stepping into the role of the person you want to become. It's like an actor learning their lines: they immerse themselves in that character, feel all of its facets and the life it has. They become that person, and it feels completely natural.

"You are doing the same thing. You decide who you want to be. Look around you: who do you admire and why? What aspects of their character do you want to develop in yourself?

It's not necessary to copy the whole person; take the part of them that you want to cultivate within yourself.

"What I did myself was visualize how and who I wanted to be without compromising my own values. I wrote it down.

"I enjoy writing things out, because it makes the situation clearer for myself. Studies have shown that we absorb information much better when we write things down on paper. We can reread them, and the new ideas don't vanish into thin air.

"Of course, you can also use your computer, but it seems to be slightly less effective. It has to do with how the mind works, with the movement of writing and the eyes. Don't ask me exactly how it works; I haven't studied it. Writing these thoughts down on paper also gives me a sense of really taking some time for myself.

"Then I searched in autobiographies, on social media, and on the Internet for people who had the characteristic that I wanted to develop within myself. I integrated this new image into myself until it felt natural, and I became the woman I am today. It has become a part of me.

"You might wonder: isn't it fake to copy someone else? My answer to that is no. Look at who you have become today. Where does that come from? It's already a mixture of the people around you (in addition to what you have added yourself through the situations you were in and your own thoughts and feelings). In other words, you can use this same process to become the person you want to be, with your own values. You apply it to all aspects of your life.

"Let's take another example. Max, you love playing the piano. Picture a well-known person in your mind who plays effortlessly for a large audience. See how confidently he walks onto the stage. Look at his posture; see how he moves. Notice how he naturally interacts with the audience, how he looks around and makes eye contact. He exudes self-assurance. See him take his place behind the grand piano and play his favorite piece with confidence. Imagine what must have happened for him to become the man he is today. Maybe the first time he stepped onto the stage, he had shaky knees and could barely look at the audience. But he saw how colleagues around him effortlessly handled that situation, and he copied their behavior and demeanor. Bit by bit, he gained more self-confidence. You see, it's something very natural.

"Let's talk about self-confidence. It's a word we use, but often we don't realize what it truly means. It's the confidence in your 'self': you are the 'self.' It's the image you have of yourself and how you think about yourself, how you talk to yourself. Is it positive and constructive or not?

"We naturally have self-confidence when we are very young, but then we are shaped by our environment, through the negative comments we receive or by unconsciously copying someone in our immediate surroundings who lacks self-confidence.

"*Most of us have lost that natural self-confidence, but it's never too late to regain it.*

"What helped me gain more self-confidence, or rather regain it, was forming a positive image of myself. As I mentioned, it was the image of the woman I wanted to be.

"The first thing I did was start walking with a straighter posture. Being 5 feet, seven inches tall, I was the second tallest girl in my class, and even here in France, I am a tall woman compared to most. Especially when wearing heels," I add with a laugh. "I had developed the habit of making myself smaller by walking with a rounded back. Until I consciously started standing tall and straight: shoulders back, head held high, pelvis tilted forward. That already felt very different, and I also started walking 10 percent faster, which gives more energy and dynamism.

"Second, I decided not to worry about what others think of me. Because you know what? They don't think about others; they are too busy with themselves and asking themselves the same questions. Isn't that funny? I'd been stressing about this for years for no reason, for something that only took place in my own thoughts.

"The third step was to stop criticizing myself. I was truly a champion at putting myself down. You wouldn't believe the way I talked to myself. Those are things you wouldn't even say to your worst enemy. It's not an excuse, but through working with many clients, I've discovered that I'm not the only one who treats themselves this way. It's almost like a global epidemic," I add sadly. "For me, it was a very persistent habit, and I often wasn't even aware of it.

"Sometimes habits are invisible to ourselves but noticeable to others. To become more aware of how many times a day I had a negative comment about myself, I wore a rubber band around my wrist for a certain period of time. Every time I caught myself making a negative comment, I would pull on the rubber band and release it against my wrist (not too hard, of course). The intention was not to hurt or punish myself. It simply served the purpose of creating awareness. At first I was shocked, truly shocked, by the number of times I used the elastic band, and I felt deeply saddened by the way I treated myself. On the other hand, this insight was incredibly valuable in transforming an old, bad habit into a good, positive one. That's when the real work could begin."

21

You Are the Thinker

"That's interesting what you're telling me, Helena, about the rubber band," Max replies. "It's something I want to try. Some kids in my class use it when they need to remember something. It's nice because it doesn't stand out much if I wear one. Can you tell me more about thinking, though? I understand it's very important."

"I've already mentioned that verse from the Bible: 'As a man thinks, so he is.' I want to add that the *words* he uses also define him. How often do you hear someone say, 'Oh, how stupid I am!' and so on? Our thoughts are powerful. With them, we make or break our own world. We are in control of our own thoughts, and the good news is that we can change them."

"If you say to yourself, 'I am fat; I am dumb; I can't do this,' you are incarcerating yourself in your self-created prison, and your mind (or as we call it, your consciousness) will provide numerous examples to confirm the negative image.

"I mentioned before that there are different natural or universal laws, and the law of thinking is one of them.

"To become aware of what you think, you can write it down:

"*How do I think about myself?*

"*How do I see myself?*

"*What do I appreciate about myself?*

"*What do I not appreciate about myself?*

"*What criticisms do I have of myself, and what words do I use then?*

"It's important to discover who you are, what abilities and qualities you have. I've mentioned it before: ask yourself the question: What brings me joy? And do more of it.

"I've already said that you have to be your own best friend. That has everything to do with how you think about yourself, how you treat yourself. The better and more positively you treat yourself, the less stress you have. Less stress enables you to feel relaxed, at ease, confident. It's like a virtuous circle.

"You always have the choice to change. You can beat yourself up because, for example, you got a bad grade in French. But you can also ask yourself the following question: 'Did I do everything necessary to get a good grade?' Be honest with yourself by saying, 'It is my own responsibility and mine alone to get a good grade.'

"You can also say, 'I hate learning languages, even learning to write my own language correctly.' Take it a step further and ask yourself, 'What do I gain from this thought?'

"You can answer with, 'I don't have to invest any more time in it. I can watch TV, play games on the computer, chat with friends, or whatever.'

"Then ask yourself, 'What do I lose as a result?' Losses can include constantly berating yourself or feeling dumb, insecure, feeling less than others. This last one has far-reaching consequences because you will not only feel dumb in French, but also in other subjects. This thought also affects your future, your professional career. How many people are brilliant but underperform?"

I see Max looking gloomy. "Why don't we learn these kinds of things in school: how to communicate with each other, self-confidence, how to interact with others?"

I look at him understandingly. "You're right. School is a learning environment, and I believe this should be a part of it. Look at the wise men of Babylon. They passed on all their knowledge regarding natural laws and universal laws: how to deal with money, trade, running your own business, culture, your relationship with people—in short, about life.

"The educational system believes that this is the parents' responsibility, but we can't expect it from them unless they themselves have embarked on the path of personal development; in that case, they can pass it on to us. But they cannot teach us what they themselves have not learned from their own parents. That doesn't mean they fall short as parents. They always do their best with the knowledge they have at that time.

"It is my dream for the future that the education system will change and focus more on current needs and the future. In my experience, the present system is outdated. A different approach to teaching is needed. I have a vision for the future in which teachers feel like leaders of their classrooms; they are respected. Children look forward to learning and discovering new things. Students collaborate and form a brotherhood. I know you can't be friends with everyone, but I hope for mutual respect and acceptance, where everyone is seen as a human being and not judged based on labels such as color, nationality, or gender, or whether you're seen as gifted or dumb or as having a certain disability.

"Every child is unique. Every person is unique, and we all have our own qualities. It is important to have space to discover and develop these unique qualities. We were not created to all be the same.

"Imagine, Max, if we all had the same appearance and did the same things. The world would be boring. The developments of the last century would never have taken place. There would be no airplanes, no mobile phones, no Internet, no electric lighting, no hot water. We would still be living like the first people on earth.

"Every person on this earth is important. We all know that one person can change the whole world. Let's develop our unique talents. There is no competition, because no one is the same, and there is enough room for everyone.

"I believe it is important to know our own value: that way, we can also appreciate the value of others. In my opinion, we can start doing that playfully at an early age. From the age of five or six, children are still open and receptive. Let's fill their minds with good things; after all, their minds will eventually be filled with good and not-so-good things anyway."

The evening is beginning to fall, and I see that Max's head is spinning from all the information.

"I think it's time to stop our conversation for today, Max. It's starting to get dark outside, and I believe you still have homework waiting for you."

"No, luckily not," says Max. "When I come to see you, I make sure that most, if not everything, is already done. I know from experience that my thoughts go in all directions. You give me so much valuable material that I need some time to process it."

I look at him with a smile. "Yes, once I get started talking, it's hard to stop me. But what do you expect with over thirty years of experience? And I'm still learning every day. Our conversations remind me of the fundamental things that are necessary. I enjoy adding them back into my daily routine. Shall we meet again in two days? I will be out of town tomorrow for a coaching client. Morning or afternoon?"

"Afternoon, please."

"Great. See you in two days then."

I hear him pause and take a deep breath as he walks out the front door. Then he continues on his way to the garden gate.

22

Vision Board

On Saturday, I wake up early to do my meditation. There has been a frost, and everything has acquired a beautiful white transparent color. Just one more month, and it will be Christmas again. Today I will bring down the Christmas decorations from the attic. Maybe Max will feel like helping me.

I love Christmas and its decorations. It makes the house so cozy. It's a delight to walk through the city. It looks like a fairy tale, with Christmas decorations stretching from one side of the street to the other and beautiful Christmas ornaments on the main squares. The city breathes a completely different atmosphere. But the highlight is the city center. The main square and the side streets have been transformed into a winter wonderland. There are cozy wooden huts selling all kinds of Christmas gifts and serving hot chocolate or mulled wine. Enormous Christmas trees stand tall. Santa Claus has his own little house where children can have their photo taken with him.

There is also an outdoor ice-skating rink. It's great fun for young and old alike, since even the little ones can enjoy themselves while being pushed on by a skating parent, sibling, or friend. I think the ice slide is the biggest hit, which you zoom down on a large rubber tube. It makes me happy to see how parents have fun with their children. I don't know who enjoys it more, the parents or the kids. Parents become kids again.

I have retrieved my Christmas decorations and am lost in thought when I hear the doorbell ring at two o'clock, and Max pushes open the front door.

"Wow, you have a healthy, rosy color," I say.

"I decided to go for a run this afternoon instead of this morning. And I slept in because Mom and I were talking late."

"I get the impression that the bond between you is starting to change."

"Yes, absolutely," Max replies. "Sometimes I don't even recognize her anymore. I think it's doing her so much good that she's losing weight. She's also dressing more nicely and occasionally humming a tune. I had never heard her do that before. Dad says she used to be cheerful and laughed a lot in the past. So I feel like she's finding herself again. She recently joined a gym and goes there three times a week."

I look at him with a smile. "I see that significant changes are happening in your home, all because one person is changing their life! The whole family is changing along with it."

"Yes, there is much more harmony in the house."

"I'm so glad to hear that, Max. Would you like to decorate the living room with me? I brought down the Christmas decorations this morning."

"Awesome," Max replies. "But isn't it a bit early to start now?"

"I know it's still a month away, but I have so many decorations and plenty of space to decorate, so I do it in stages. I'll start with the living room."

"I'd be happy to help you with that."

We get to work. It's so cozy to do it together. I can see that Max is enjoying it too. "Do you always help your mother with the Christmas decorations?" I ask.

"We don't do much about it usually. We have an artificial tree that we put away in the garage with the decorations still on, so there's not much to do. Then we hang a few decorations here and there. It's quite different at your place. But your house is much bigger."

After an hour and a half of hard work, the living room is transformed and unrecognizable. To judge by Max's face, he likes the result. Once we've put away the boxes, we sit down on the couch to enjoy some hot chocolate and the beautiful decorations.

"Referring back to our last conversation, Max: about who you are, who you want to be, what you want, what you want to have, and how you see yourself. I use an exercise myself for that, and I call it 'My Life Description.' It's very simple: First, I relax by taking a few calm and deep breaths or through meditation. Then I let my imagination run wild and start typing what I want. I find it easier to use my computer rather than writing it down because more details come up each time to make the picture perfect: exactly how I want it. I write down all the details that are important to evoke the feeling. Everything is possible, of course, within moral norms and natural laws. Besides these, there are no limitations. I don't wonder about how I can get this or how I can make it happen. I'm not concerned with that because it will only limit me in everything that is possible.

"I make sure my description covers all aspects of my life. Professional: my businesses, like my online business, coaching business, my books, my programs, my team. I also consider money: my sources of income and investments. I think about my health: physical, mental, sports, nutrition. But I also think about family: my husband, children, grandchildren, friends, and other relationships. I determine how I want to spend my free time: my vacations and outings. And I think about housing: where and how I will live. In short, everything that is important to me.

"I think about all of this in the present tense, as if I have already achieved it. I don't write 'I will have' or 'I will do,' because that belongs to the future, and the future never arrives. Your wish or vision will always remain in the future."

"Let me go back to the example I used earlier. Before I bought this house, I had a clear image of the kind of house I wanted. Which neighborhood, which surroundings, close to a forest, and all the amenities within walking distance. How many bedrooms with en suite bathrooms. A comfortable living room, a separate dining room with a long dining table for ten people. A spacious, practical kitchen where everything is at hand and you move as little as possible, with plenty of storage cabinets and a large kitchen island in the middle. In my mind, I saw myself my husband and friends having the greatest pleasure cooking delicious meals and exchanging recipes.

After the meal, we would settle on a comfortable couch to enjoy a good movie on a big screen together. On a warm day, we would enjoy some cooling off in the pool. I wrote it down in that way, with a lot of feeling and positive words."

"OK, now it's clearer what you're doing," says Max.

I continue, "Then I use an app on my phone to record my vision so that I can listen to it anywhere, while I'm cooking, walking, going to the supermarket. The secret behind materializing is repetition and feeling. I maintain the feeling of enthusiasm, excitement, and joy in having what I want throughout the day. I live it, experience it, see it, smell it, feel it, hear it. I live in the future now. Through constant repetition with the accompanying feeling, it eventually starts to feel very natural.

"I overlooked this feeling for a long time. I recited my affirmations like a robot. I mentioned my ideal life without much emotion and didn't understand why it didn't always work. This has to do with the law of attraction. The energy you emit comes back to you. You have to align yourself with the energy of what you want to achieve. That is a high energy: the energy of joy and gratitude.

"Then comes the next step: follow your intuition. Nothing will change in your life if you don't take action. Follow the inspirations you receive. It's not like you can sit in your chair hoping that what you want will come to you. You send a message to the universe by saying, 'This is what I want.' Never wonder, how can I get or afford this? The universe has its own solutions for that. I only focus on what I want and follow my inspirations to take action.

"If you want to achieve or accomplish something in your life, don't say, "If I do this or that, then I will get this or that.' Start with the end goal in mind and work backward. I've talked about this before when we discussed accepting yourself. Do you remember that, Max?"

Max nods.

"I want to come back to the fact that you're being bullied. Let's write down the ideal situation. What do you want? How do you see your life? How do you want to feel?"

"What I want is for it to stop," Max replies. He furrows his brow.

I can tell this is a difficult topic for him.

"OK, but how can you phrase that in a positive way?"

"That they leave me alone," Max answers.

"Before we continue, try to relax first, Max. I can see tension in your face as soon as we bring up the topic of bullying."

"Max sighs deeply.

"Close your eyes," I continue, "and take a few calm breaths in and out. Good, much better. Now breathe in for four counts and breathe out for eight counts. Here we go: 1, 2, 3, 4, and breathe out: 8, 7, 6, 5, 4, 3, 2, 1. Let's repeat that a few times."

I see Max slowly relaxing.

"Do you feel better, Max?"

"Yes, I feel more relaxed."

"Now let's start with the words 'I am happy and grateful now that . . .' and fill it in."

Max begins, "I am happy and grateful now that they leave me alone."

"What does it mean for you, that they leave you alone?"

"That I can be myself, that I can go wherever I want, like to the bathroom, that I can eat in the school cafeteria, cross the schoolyard. That I can take my time to get my belongings from my locker without being afraid that they will knock everything out of my hands. That I find my clothes after sports, just as I left them, and not in the shower, in the trash, damaged, or I can't find them at all. That I am accepted and not laughed at or jeered at because I am overweight."

"What else?"

"That I can say something without being laughed at."

I see that he is becoming emotional and ask if it's OK to continue. He nods.

"OK," I say, "we have a foundation to work with, and you can add to it later on your own. From what I understand, Max—and correct me if I'm wrong—you want respect for yourself and your belongings. You want to be accepted as you are."

"Yes, that sums it up in a few words," confirms Max.

"Based on the ideal situation, you could write things like: 'I am so happy and grateful now that I feel happy and relaxed, appreciated, and accepted. I am at one with myself and with others. It's wonderful to go to school every day. It's nice to meet my classmates and other students. There is a pleasant and relaxed atmosphere at school. I feel respected, and there is respect for my belongings. Learning is easy and enjoyable, and everyone is happy that I excel in most subjects. My opinion is valued. I am surrounded by warm, loving people. It's wonderful to be myself under all circumstances. People love me, and I am fully accepted for who I am. The world is a safe place to be. Every day, enjoyable and joyful things happen in my life.'"

I continue: "Let's also add something about your body. For example, think: 'I love my body, and I am grateful that it works so well day in and day out. I take loving care of it. My body knows exactly what it needs to be healthy and full of energy, and I listen to my own needs.'"

Now it becomes too much for Max. "If only all of that could be true," he says with a small voice.

"Of course it doesn't happen overnight. But buckle up, because things can sometimes happen very quickly."

Max is silent for a moment, taking it all in. "What do you want me to do with that text?" he asks.

"I want you to repeat it to yourself as much as possible every day until you truly believe it. In the beginning, it may give you a feeling of 'Maybe it's possible,' but by regularly repeating your text, you'll probably start thinking after a while, 'Yes, it is possible!' By continuing to repeat it and over-write old negative thoughts, you'll think, 'Yes, of course this is possible.' Then it will give you a feeling of certainty. That's when you are aligned with your goal. Research has shown that you need to repeat a new thought for at least twenty-five to thirty consecutive days. If you skip a day, you'll have to start over from day one.

"When you start rewriting your thoughts, you don't need to know how things will turn out. Leave that to the universe, because it arranges everything perfectly. We just need to ask for what we want and believe that we will receive it. But we must also be open to receiving it. That means being receptive. What I mean by that is never to doubt, because doubting affirms the opposite of what you want. And lastly, follow your intuition and take action.

"This version is just an example. Use your own words, but most importantly, infuse it with positive emotion and a sense of joy. Once you've written it down, extract the essence and write it on a note or card that you carry with you. Read it regularly throughout the day. It's about transforming the negative thoughts you have into positive, constructive thoughts.

"An affirmation could be: 'I fully and completely accept myself exactly as I am. I am perfect, and I am surrounded by loving, respectful people who fully and completely support and accept me.' Do you understand the purpose and how it works, Max?"

"Yes, it's becoming clearer to me, but I still don't fully understand what you mean when you talk about the universe."

"That's because it's not visible. I believe that there is a power greater than myself, a loving power. That, for me, is the universal energy that connects everything and everyone. I use the word *universe* because it's a neutral word, but you can also use the word *God* or *Allah* or any other name. It's whatever resonates with you the most. I use the words *universe* and *God* interchangeably. God, for me, is not someone sitting on a cloud all day watching if I make mistakes or punishing me for not doing something right. We punish ourselves with our conscience, the words we say to ourselves, and our fears.

"God, for me, is pure love, pure energy, harmony, happiness, and joy. When I don't feel happy and joyful, it means I have disconnected myself from this energy, which I am myself. It creates a feeling of chaos. I feel sick, tired, or stressed, and I'm not comfortable in my own skin. I know that's the moment to take a closer look at myself."

"How do you do that?" Max asks.

"What I do is very simple. I focus on my body and try to feel what it wants to tell me. I scan my body. Where is the emotion? In my stomach? In my back? Each area in my body says something about what's happening in my life. I just need to feel it and listen in order to understand it. For example, let's talk about feet. Do you remember when you were angry and kicked a big stone, and your foot started bleeding?"

"Oh yeah, I won't forget that drama easily."

"Feet," I continue, "are made for moving forward and symbolize progress in life. Are you on the right path? Is it taking you where you want to go? Do you see how simple it is to translate it? Once you understand the signal, ask yourself the following question: how can I easily move forward in life? Don't ask why in a negative way, because then your mind will come up with a lot of arguments that won't help you progress, and you'll attract more things you don't want. Avoid questions like, 'Why is this happening to me? Why do they always target me? Why are they doing this to me?'

"Instead, it's better to use *how*. By using *how*, you'll be presented with creative solutions, and that's what we want.

"Alternatively, you can use *why* in a positive way, such as: 'Why is it so easy for me to move forward in my life? Why do I easily make friendships? Why do I have a beautiful body?'

"Regarding your body, you can always find something in or about it that you can appreciate. For example: 'My heart pumps blood around without my even thinking about it. My body has a perfect mechanism for digesting food and cleansing itself. It all happens naturally. I have a lovely smiling face.' You can come up with many more.

"It's even true that if you don't listen to the initial signals from your body, it will start sending stronger signals. If there's still no response, it will send very strong signals, such as an accident or illness."

"I still find it difficult to believe, Helena."

"Take a good look around you, listen to people's stories, and you'll understand. Of course, they don't say, 'I'm going to get sick or have an accident' on purpose. They create these effects unconsciously. The body sends a signal to wake you up, to tell you that something is wrong, that you've drifted away from yourself. What your pure essence, your self, wants is to be happy, to feel joyous and uplifted, to be in love with yourself and life. It's like when you fall in love with a girl. That wonderful feeling that makes you feel like you can move mountains. You feel on top of the world. You should have that feeling for yourself because that's what your pure essence—your self—already is. In other words, the energies need to align, be in harmony with each other. If you're not in this state of joy, you're disconnected from yourself. Does this make things clearer for you, Max?"

"I'm starting to understand it bit by bit."

"You know," I say, "the good news is that happiness is within you. *You* are the only person who can make yourself happy; no one else can do that for you. You don't need to seek love outside of yourself."

"But how can I find it?"

"Simple: be your own best friend. People will react differently to you when you have respect for yourself. You love yourself and accept yourself, and you establish your boundaries. *Love yourself unconditionally.* Take, for example, the love or affection you feel for your best friend, or your father, mother, a loved one, or even a teacher or a pet. Someone or something you care deeply about. Give the same feeling that you have for those others to yourself.

"We haven't been taught that, and often it's said that it's strange to love oneself. But what's strange about it? Is it OK to love someone else but not yourself? Isn't that strange? Besides, we can't love someone else if we don't know what love is. If we're not capable of giving it to ourselves in a natural way, how can we give it to someone else?

"It has nothing to do with selfishness or vanity. Love is healing, and everyone needs it. Everything that lives on our planet needs love; we cannot do without it. Have you ever noticed that plants die in a negative and stressful environment? As I mentioned before, babies die if they don't receive love. So why would we cut ourselves off from the love we can give ourselves? Love is essential. Furthermore, if you don't give yourself love, you won't recognize it when someone else offers you love. You'll brush off a kind, sincere compliment because you don't believe it, because you don't recognize it.

"To feel this love for myself, I use the mirror when I say my affirmations. I look at myself in the mirror and say them with a lot of feeling. I repeat that every day until I reach the ideal conditions, and then I continue doing it in a shortened version. In your case, it could be something like, 'I am surrounded by loving people. I am loving and loved. The world is a safe place to live in.' Or whatever feels right for you.

"Working on yourself is a lifelong process. In the beginning, I thought, 'We write the new affirmation a few times, and poof, it sticks, and my life magically changes.' But the reality is different. Sometimes a program is so deeply ingrained in our hard drive that it takes a long time to overwrite it."

I think of something to make it even clearer for him. "Come with me, Max. I want to show you something."

We walk to the other side of the house, where one of my favorite rooms is located. We open the door to my office, and a sea of sunlight greets us. The room has soft, calm colors, and my large oak desk stands beautifully in it. I open a cabinet door, and Max stares at all the pictures I have stuck inside.

"What is that?" he asks, looking at me curiously.

"That's a vision board. As you can see, it's a collection of pictures, photos, and objects that fit the life I imagine for myself."

"It looks fabulous, Helena."

"Yes," I say, laughing. "They say, 'you create your own reality.' So I'd better have big dreams, because life will go on anyway. It's better to create my own reality exactly as I want it. Here's how it works: before I bought my dream house, I had a picture of my ideal home stuck on this board. Whatever you give your attention to grows. The result is that the house I live in now is even more perfect than I could have ever imagined. You can see other pictures here of my career, relationships, car, workshops, and vacations in the most beautiful places on earth. And a picture of a slim, healthy body."

"I see that you want to swim with dolphins," Max points and laughs at a picture of a woman in the water with a child in her arms, receiving a kiss from a dolphin.

"That's high on my list. It would be amazing to swim with those superintelligent creatures. I like printing out the pictures and hanging them in a visible spot for me. But you can also save them on the computer and view them regularly there.

"A vision board is actually nothing strange. Just think about how many teenagers have a big poster of their idol hanging in their bedroom. They want to be like their idol: singing, walking, being famous, traveling the world, owning a beautiful house, and driving flashy cars. What they have is essentially a vision board. So I guess I'm just a teenager too."

We both burst into laughter.

"Every morning when I'm home, I open the cabinet door and spend a few minutes looking at my pictures and feeling what it's like to have what is depicted in the photos. I know it's coming; I just don't know exactly when. Like with my house:

I gave myself one year to find my dream home in the perfect location. I left it up to the universe to decide where. That energy knew my criteria. I started visiting houses. Seven months later, I visited this house and instantly fell in love. It has everything and even more than I wanted. It became available because the previous occupant started working for another company and wanted to live in the south of the country.

"Sometimes what you want may not be immediately available and it takes time. During that time, you have to trust that what you want—or even something better—will come. It's the journey towards your goal that is the most exciting. It should be an enjoyable time. Once you have what you want, you'll want to achieve your next goal. In essence, we are always on our way to a goal."

We gaze at the pictures I have put up, and I continue my explanation.

"Compare your belief in achieving your goal to the belief a farmer has when growing crops. He cultivates the land. You play with the thought of what you desire. Then he sows his seeds and believes they will sprout. You start believing in the intention you have and plant your thoughts. Then nature takes over by providing the seeds with soil, water, and sunshine—the ideal conditions for germination. You do the same with your affirmation, repeating it with a lot of feeling and regularly looking at the picture on your vision board. Or you listen to the story of your ideal life. The sprouts emerge from the ground, just as your project takes shape and impulses to act arise. In my case, I had the impulse to look at houses on the Internet, and that led me to attract the right real estate agent.

"The farmer continues to believe in his crops and envisions an abundant harvest in his mind. In my case, I visited houses while holding my ideal picture in mind. I also kept saying to the universe: 'This is what I want, or something better.' Like the farmer, I had complete faith that it would work out. Eventually, the day of harvest arrives, and the harvest is greater than the farmer imagined it would be. For me, it was the day I signed the purchase contract for a house that is more beautiful than I could have dreamed of.

"Imagine if the farmer had sowed his seeds and dug them up every week to see where the plants were. And each time he said, 'Stupid seeds, why don't you give me a beautiful, big plant?' The seeds would only weaken and eventually die. The same happens to our intentions when we are impatient. Trust that it will work out. Sometimes things can come to you very quickly, and sometimes it takes a bit longer.

"Let's go back to the teenagers and their posters of idols. The same applies there. It's a shame that they only fantasize and allow themselves to be discouraged by their surroundings. Their surroundings tell them they are dreamers. And they let go of their dreams. But in fact the greatest dreamers have created the most fantastic things. What if the teenagers had held the image in their minds with great feeling? If you follow the impulses and act upon them, I am convinced that everyone is capable of great things."

I can see from Max's face that his thoughts are already drifting to images in his mind.

"I see that you like the idea of making one too," I say to Max, teasingly.

"This is cool. It seems like fun to do," he responds.

As we walk back to the living room, I ask Max how his piano lessons are going.

"They're going great. I really enjoy it, even learning to read sheet music."

"And you're still practicing on the piano at the music school?"

"Yes," says Max, "it takes some organizing, but so far, it's working out fine. By the way, Helena, if you don't mind, I'd like to go home now. I've been so inspired by your vision board that I feel like making one for myself."

"I completely understand," I say with a laugh. "It's very inspiring and a lot of fun to do."

He grabs his jacket and gives me a warm hug.

"Thank you for everything, Helena. Thank you for your time and knowledge. You are a great gift in my life, and I want to let you know that."

"Thank you, dear. The pleasure is mutual. It's heartwarming to see how you're changing. Go on now and create beautiful things for yourself."

I hear the familiar whistle again as he walks towards the garden gate. In my mind, a little plan starts to hatch.

23

Morning Ritual

The next day, Max visits again.

"So have you found any pictures for your vision board?" I ask him.

"Yes, I've started. It's really fun to do."

As we settle comfortably, Max asks me, "How do you start your day? You've told me about different exercises, but what do you actually do yourself? What works for you?"

"First of all, I make a plan for a longer period, professionally and personally, and I translate that into a daily plan. I write it out in my agenda the night before, so I know exactly what's on the agenda and can start right away. This way I don't waste time figuring out what to do. It gives me guidance and a solid foundation, and helps me to persevere. A plan in your head is not a plan. If it's not on paper, it won't get done. I've learned this from experience. I thought I could do without an agenda, but I wasn't very productive. You have so much time ahead of you that you don't know what to do with it. Then you're quickly tempted to look at social media and before you know it, one or two hours have passed.

"In the morning, before getting up, I start with a gratitude exercise. Gratitude is one of the most important things. When you're grateful, you can't be depressed. You feel good, and you attract more good things. I'm grateful for everything I have, what I am, and what happens in my life. I thank my bed for a comfortable night. There are people in the world who don't have a bed and sleep on the streets. I have a comfortable bed. Then I scan my body and thank it for functioning so well: my lungs, which have been breathing all night without me consciously having to think about it. I thank the organs that have digested my food throughout the night, my heart that has pumped blood around my body. I thank my feet, which take me everywhere. And I express gratitude for this new day, for all the pleasant surprises, companionship, and prosperity.

Then I put on my workout clothes, drink lukewarm water with lemon to cleanse my body, and do my meditation."

"What exactly is meditation, and why do you do it?"

"That's a great question, Max. I started meditation a few years ago because I was tired of myself. I had this constant urge to think. My mind was always busy, which was very exhausting. I was looking for a solution, and meditation is a great solution for that. Meditation is very simple: its purpose is to quiet the mind or bring it to rest, because our mind is constantly thinking, with about 60,000 thoughts swirling through our heads each day."

"So many?" Max exclaims.

"Impressive, isn't it? If a glass is filled with water, there's no room for more water. It's the same with our minds. If it's already filled with thoughts, the inspiration coming from within has no space to be heard. We end up living on autopilot."

"How do you empty your mind?"

"I start by settling myself in a comfortable chair and setting a timer for fifteen minutes. Then I close my eyes and focus on the ticking of the timer. Of course, in the beginning, my thoughts wander all over the place, but each time, I bring my attention back to the ticking of the timer and focus solely on that.

"It took about a month before my thoughts started to calm down during meditation, and the moments of silence became longer. Overall, I felt much calmer throughout the day, which motivated me to continue. Now meditation has become such a habit that I can't do without it anymore.

"There are different ways to meditate. For example, you can also practice walking meditation."

"What's that exactly?"

"You concentrate 100 percent on your feet. You place one foot on the ground to start walking and feel the contact with the earth. Then, very consciously, you place your other foot in front of you, feel the contact with the ground again, and take step after step. I tried this form, but I felt exhausted after a short walk. However, some people find it enjoyable.

"You can also go into nature and sit against a tree. You feel the energy of the tree and concentrate 100 percent on your breath. It's nice to connect with a monotonous sound. With music, there's a risk of starting to sing or hum along."

"OK, that doesn't sound difficult at all. I had a bit of a strange image of it. For me, it was something that monks do for hours with a special ritual."

I burst out laughing. "I used to have the exact same idea. After my meditation, I do some exercise. I have a method that I really enjoy. It combines yoga exercises with classical ballet. It strengthens my back and improves my posture. Then I do the mirror exercise. It gives me a good feeling. After that, I grab my notebook and write my affirmation seven times to change my paradigm. Then I write down my goal seven times.

"Next, I proceed to write about how grateful I am for everything. I start with: 'I am happy and grateful for . . .' and I fill it in with, for example: 'my success,' 'the money flowing into my life forever,' 'my thriving businesses,' 'my dream team,' 'my relationship with my husband and loved ones.' I can also be grateful for a beautiful sunny day. I write down a maximum of five things.

"Then I write about what I want to focus on positively for a certain period, but at least a month. If I feel I've been consuming too much sugar again, I could focus on my eating habits. I write down one positive thing about my eating habits each day and how I've nourished myself. This way, I'm consciously taking steps towards achieving the desired goal instead of criticizing myself all day for having a bloated stomach. This exercise helps me. I can also choose topics like friendships or money.

"It's a fantastic exercise. We've talked about it often: where you focus your attention positively, that's where it grows. It makes me happy, especially when I read it back, to see how well I'm progressing. For you, a good exercise would be to concentrate on something positive you notice about your bully every day."

"Positive," Max says mockingly. "What positive thing can I see in my bully?"

"Of course, it takes a lot of concentration in the beginning, but you can write down something positive that is true for you. Like: 'He is the leader of the group,' and don't dwell on the details. Absolutely do not write down negative things. It could be that he was wearing a nice sweater that day or new sneakers. Or he always looks well-groomed. Find something positive. If I were you, I would definitely do this for a while. You will feel what is needed. It could be a few months, but you will see that the energy between you will change."

"That's quite intense—to see your enemy in a positive light."

"I understand your reluctance, but you will see that this is a very powerful exercise with results that you can't even imagine right now.

"To continue with my morning ritual: Lastly, I read a positive book for half an hour, a book that I am studying at that moment. Then I'm ready to start my day."

24

Forgiveness

"Max, we have talked about many different things by now. We started with nutrition. We discussed the law of attraction: what we emit comes back to us. We looked at the story we tell ourselves, our self-image, and the impact on our self-confidence. The law of thinking: what we think about ourselves and the world, our communication with ourselves, how we talk about and to ourselves. We have discussed various techniques: meditation, breathing exercises to relax, writing down goals, describing our ideal life. We talked about creating affirmations and writing them down every day, visualization, vision boards, the mirror exercise, gratitude exercises. And you do all of this with the same goal: learning to love yourself.

"I want to add a forgiveness exercise. I struggled with this, because I thought it was condoning behavior that was unacceptable. But the purpose is not to justify what happened, but to free ourselves from the emotions we hold on to. Sometimes we continue to hurt ourselves for ten or twenty years, or even longer, by repeatedly bringing back thoughts about something that happened at some point in the past. We evoke the pain and stress as if it is still happening now.

"The body doesn't distinguish between a memory of something that happened in the past and what is happening now. That's why forgiveness is an act of self-love. You don't have to talk to the person who has done something hurtful to you, but if you feel the need, it's OK. In principle, a simple sheet of paper is enough.

"You start with: 'Dear . . .' and you fill in the name of the person, or it can be yourself that you want to forgive. Then you write down why you are angry: write it out in all the details, let yourself go completely. After that, note what you missed and what you would have liked to receive. Write down what you are grateful for as well. Finally, write: 'I forgive you because you are not how I wanted you to be. I forgive you; I set you free. And I forgive myself. You are free, and I am free, and I let you go.'

"My experience is that it is necessary to forgive the same person multiple times before the emotion completely fades away. It's like cleaning away layer by layer.

"Another way of forgiving is to put your bully on a stage and you, as the spectator, say everything you want to say to him. Let it all out. It is absolutely safe to do so. He only listens, and you continue until you've said everything. Close the scene with the words: 'I forgive you because you are not how I wanted you to be, I forgive you, I set you free, and I forgive myself.'

"What do you mean by 'I set you free'?" Max asks. "Setting someone free means there is no more negative energy that binds you together. It is what you say to the universe: 'I let go; I am no longer attached to this energy.'

"You need to rise above the bully. You have to outsmart them, but in a respectful way. Don't respond to violence with violence, as it will only make things worse. Children who act as clowns and make jokes about themselves are not bullied. Max, understand that no one can destroy you. It's your feelings about the situation that give you the fearful and uncomfortable feeling.

Practice at home with some responses you can give to the bully. You don't have to figure it out all by yourself. Maybe your best friend can help—the one who knows what's been happening. Ask him to play the bully for a moment and throw a few comments your way, so you can try out different reactions. It's not about being perfect—it's about getting used to speaking calmly, without freezing or shrinking.

"If you'd like, you can also practice with me. We can go through a few situations together until it starts to feel more natural. We'll take it slow. There's no pressure.

"Also, try practicing in front of the mirror. Look yourself in the eyes as you say your responses. Not with anger, but with calm, steady confidence. At first, it might feel awkward or silly—but over time, something shifts. You begin to see someone strong looking back at you."

Max was quiet for a moment, then said, "I think I'd like to try it in front of the mirror first. Just to get used to saying something. And maybe later I could ask my friend. Or you."

I go on: "When you talk to the bully, look them straight in the eyes, speak calmly and peacefully, and then continue on your way.

"Here's how it goes: you catch the boomerang of the hurtful words from your bully and throw it back with a positive or neutral remark. An example is: 'Hey, pig, you stink.' Catch the boomerang and throw it back. Look your bully in the eyes and say, 'Ah, that's my natural perfume.' This breaks his words and leaves him speechless. He'll be completely embarrassed if members of his group laugh at him. He'll be guaranteed to leave you alone and may seek another victim.

"See if you can make the edited photos of yourself that appear on social media even funnier. Post them with a caption like, 'Ha, ha, that's hilarious.' Or, 'Thanks for spreading this funny photo. I had a good laugh.' Or, 'I feel like a king with all this attention.' Find creative responses, and prepare well. They should flow smoothly and effortlessly. Generally you only get one chance to give a good comeback.

"How can you best deal with anger? When I was very angry and frustrated, I was advised to buy a punching bag to take out my aggression, or use my pillow to hit and scream out my aggression. It works fantastically, I must say, but I only screamed when no one else was home. Sometimes I would drive to a quiet place to scream loudly. I discovered that I can also do it in the car when it's parked in the garage, because no one hears me.

"It's normal and acceptable to get angry. It's up to us to find a way to balance the increased adrenaline that is released as a result. Many people do this through exercise. By the way, running is also very enjoyable."

"I absolutely agree," Max responds. "Running has done me a lot of good. When I'm angry, I run harder and often go an extra lap to change my thoughts."

"I also have an evening ritual to help me relax and sleep. I try not to work on the computer after nine o'clock, which I manage to do most days. Then I read a bit, or I watch an interesting documentary, or I listen to an audiobook. I don't watch TV, and I don't listen to the news, because it's negative, and I don't want to carry that into my sleep.

"Before going to sleep, I reflect on the day moment by moment. What went well that day? And I give myself compliments for it. I also look at what didn't go well. What can I learn from it, and how can I do better next time? Once a moment has been reviewed, I imagine throwing it over my shoulder with a shovel. I consider it finished. As a result, I can sleep well and relax.

"Together with all the techniques that we discussed earlier and you are already implementing, this will surely change your self-image. Have you noticed anything in your surroundings?"

"Yes, I have the impression that people are responding to me differently. Nicer."

"That's fantastic, Max. I'm very happy to hear that."

25

Surprise

A week later, I call Max to ask if he can come over. I have a gift for him, and I'd like to give it to him before Christmas.

"Yes, of course," Max replies. "I have a short day at school next Wednesday, so I can stop by at four o'clock. I just can't stay long because I have a few tests that I still want to review for."

I say, "That's fine."

Max is wrapped up when he comes to me on Wednesday. "Is it that cold outside?" I ask him.

"Yes, the temperature dropped a lot today. It was freezing this morning. I didn't realize it, but once I started my paper route, I got super cold and couldn't warm up. That's why I pulled out my thickest coat. Oh," Max continues, "I see you've continued with the decorations. How cozy. I'll convince my mom to make it cozy at our place too."

Once we're seated, I ask him how his vision board is going.

"You know what's funny? In the beginning, when I wondered what I would like to have or do, it was difficult for me to come up with something. Then I imagined Aladdin's lamp, rubbed it in my mind, and repeated to myself: 'Anything is possible; there are no limitations. I can wish for whatever I want. These are my gifts. What makes me happy?' Little by little, my wishes started appearing on paper. Then I looked for matching pictures, which I critically examined one by one to see if they met all the criteria. And it worked, but just like you said, once you get the hang of it, you think, oh, that's also nice, and that too. It's growing almost daily."

"What a great idea to imagine it like that with Aladdin's lamp. That's funny!"

"Yes, it was really fun. By the way, didn't I tell you that I can't stay long? I don't want to be rude."

"Yes, I know, you mentioned it beforehand. Will you walk with me for your gift?"

We go to my office where a large box is transformed into a fireplace mantle with Christmas decorations on it and a few small presents around it.

"You've made it cozy even here in your office," Max says. "What a great idea to create a fireplace mantle! It's really cute. Are all these presents for me?" he asks excitedly.

I nod with a big smile. He starts eagerly unwrapping the gifts. In the first one, there's a T-shirt with the text, "Max is the greatest." He laughs. "That'll come in handy: I can use it when I go for a run."

Then there are a few more small presents. Once those are unwrapped, I say to Max, "Unfortunately, now we'll have to break apart the beautiful fireplace mantle because there's also a gift inside. Here, I have a knife and scissors for you. Be careful not to damage the contents."

Max hesitates to break apart the fireplace mantle. "Is there any way we can keep the cardboard intact? I could put it up at home."

"Give it a try."

Max carefully starts removing the top and carefully cuts through the tape holding the box together. He's focused on preserving the decorations as much as possible. Then he opens the lid of the box, and he bursts into tears. "It's not true," he sobs. "It's not true. And I just put the picture of it on my vision board yesterday. Helena, I've never received such a big gift in my life. It must have cost a fortune." Suddenly, paying no more attention to the box, he tears it apart into large pieces.

In front of him is a beautiful black electric piano. Max is speechless and gazes at it in disbelief. "Helena, it's beautiful," he says in a soft voice, and he lovingly runs his hand over the keys. Then he turns around, wraps his arms around me, and gives me a big hug. "Thank you, Helena, thank you. I can't find the words. I'm incredibly happy with it. I have to ask my mom if there's space for it in the lounge. You see, we don't have much room."

"Just ask," I say. "Hopefully, there's a spot. In the meantime, I'll give you the keys to my house so you can come whenever you want. We'll put it in the small living room so that you have space and can play undisturbed. There's also a headphone included. Look, it's here in the box."

"I have to go," Max says, a bit downcast. "But I want to play something first. I can't focus on that test now."

"Uh-oh, that's not a good sign," I tease him.

We together carry the piano to the small living room. "Max, for now, you'll have to use my old office chair because I haven't bought a piano stool yet. I think it's better to do that together since it's something very personal."

"A desk chair is fine," Max replies.

After I retrieve the chair from the garage, Max takes a seat at the piano. "I can't play much yet," he apologizes. "I've just started."

"Play what you know," I say as I sit on the couch.

The music is a bit messy, but you can't expect too much from someone who has just begun. It's already a delight to watch him. His face is beaming from ear to ear. After ten minutes, he stops. "Helena, I don't know how I can ever thank you."

I look at him playfully. "Weren't you the one who rubbed Aladdin's lamp and made this wish?"

"But you didn't know anything about it. How is that possible?"

"See, that's the law of vibration and synchronicity. So be careful what you ask the universe for," I add with a wink. We laugh together.

"I'm really going to enjoy this," Max says. "Helena, I have to go. Thank you a thousand times."

"Here are the keys," I say, presenting them to him with an official gesture. "Come whenever you want to play."

26

Concert

I am sitting in one of the best seats in the grand hall of the beautiful Concertgebouw in Amsterdam. The elegant space is slowly filling up. I am excited and grateful to be able to attend this special evening. Fifteen years have passed since I first met Max, and so much has happened! Time has flown by. Max has changed so much. I can hardly recognize him. What a difference from how I found him back then. I am very proud of what he has become. He has always kept his goal in mind, and his passion for music has become his life. For him, it doesn't even feel like work, but pure enjoyment to do what he loves most, which is performing piano concerts. He is one of the world's most renowned and sought-after pianists. Today thousands of people have gathered to celebrate his success with a special concert.

It has been a long journey, but Max has worked hard on himself. When he was feeling down and lost, he would call me by phone to lift his spirits. Those calls became rarer and rarer, which was, of course, a good sign. It has been several years since I last saw him. He now travels the world and has won numerous international awards. I am looking forward to seeing him again. We have agreed to have dinner together after the concert. The buzz around me grows louder and louder.

Earlier this afternoon, I had my first meeting with Max's parents. It was very emotional. They thanked me warmly for everything I have meant to Max. Only recently did he share with them the darkest period of his life. It was only then that his parents realized where that sudden turnaround in Max's life came from: when he wanted to lose weight, took on a paper route, started piano lessons, and wanted to go to the conservatory in Paris. They felt guilty for never having seen how unhappy their son was during that time, how he was bullied at school. But it eased their pain to know that there was someone he could rely on then and still can.

I see famous people all around me taking their seats. A beautiful Steinway piano stands in the center of the stage, ready to be played by loving hands. After a short speech by the organizer, Max steps onto the stage, slim and sharp in his suit. He looks fantastic. Thunderous applause erupts. He takes his place behind the piano, focuses for a few moments, and then effortlessly glides his fingers over the keys in a rapid tempo. He occasionally closes his eyes and completely immerses himself in the music. I always find it beautiful to see people play with such passion, when their whole body becomes one with the music. My body responds in the same way, slowly swaying back and forth. Max has chosen a magnificent piece, and at the end he receives a long standing ovation. After a brief ceremony, he accepts the world's highest music award, the culmination of his years of hard work.

We meet an hour later in the restaurant of the hotel where he is staying and we embrace each other, crying. What an emotional reunion! Once I regain my voice, I congratulate him on his achieved success. He smiles and replies, "You pushed me so hard. I couldn't do otherwise." We both burst into laughter.

A table is reserved by the window, where we have a beautiful view of the canal. I love this view. I love my beloved Amsterdam, a city like no other in the world. We order a light dinner, and I ask Max, "Tell me, how have things been all these years we haven't seen each other?"

"If I have to tell you everything, we won't finish talking anytime soon," Max replies. "But in broad strokes, this is it. When I went to the conservatory in Paris, I truly felt I was in the right place. I was surrounded by people with the same passion. I kept working on myself constantly. It's like you said: it's a lifelong process, and the journey towards your goal is the most important part. I immensely enjoyed the journey to my success. I constantly worked on what I no longer wanted and replaced my old routines with good habits that propelled me forward.

"But the major breakthrough came when I did the forgiveness exercise regarding my bully several times. I immediately saw significant developments in my success and personal life. I freed myself from the prison I had created for myself. I felt liberated, and nothing and no one could stop me. I no longer blocked myself. I always had a clear vision of my ultimate goal, which was to be the best and highest-paid concert pianist on earth.

"Another breakthrough in working on myself was when I reached out to my bully. You said it wasn't necessarily required to have contact with the person you want to forgive, but I felt I needed that. I called him, and he was surprised to hear my voice. I thanked him for what had happened during that time. There was silence on the phone for a long time, and then I continued the conversation, telling him that without his bullying, I probably wouldn't be the person I am today. I don't know if he cried on the phone, but his voice didn't have the same volume anymore. He told me how sorry he was for making me his target and shared details about his childhood and how his parents treated him. I won't go into details because it's not uplifting. I invited him to a concert, and he gratefully accepted. I saw him standing in the distance in the hall. He chose not to shake my hand, and that was OK. For me, it was about closing a chapter. He didn't have to come to me to greet me. When you give, give from your heart without expecting anything in return, you always used to say, and it gives a good feeling.

"You see," he adds with a smile, "I'm a good student. I still make time for my morning routine every day. I couldn't live without all of this anymore. If I skipped it for one day, I would miss it. It's like brushing your teeth: you do it automatically, because it's good for you. Without it, I wouldn't be where I am today in my personal and professional life.

"Another thing I pay attention to for maintaining optimal health is my nutrition. I'm very particular about the restaurants I choose or that are chosen for me. I don't want to eat fries or rice every evening with a leaf of lettuce alongside my meat or fish. The kitchen must use fresh, preferably organic, vegetables.

"I'm grateful for all the wonderful things that have happened in my life," Max continues, "but one of the most beautiful gifts is my wife. We have a relationship where we are deeply connected. In the beginning, we talked a lot to discover how each of us is programmed and what our mutual beliefs are, and now we are completely on the same wavelength. It's very easy to listen to each other and communicate. There is deep mutual trust and a profound love bond between us. It's a joy to be together. It's exactly as I had imagined," he says with a wink towards me. "She was in the story I had written for my life."

I burst into laughter.

"Yes, that story gives you a clear vision of how you want your life to be. Your wife is a highly sought-after opera singer, isn't she? How do you make sure you see each other regularly? Doesn't it have a negative impact on your relationship when you're away for extended periods?"

"As I told you," Max continues, "we are on the same wavelength, and our relationship is very important. It's more important than our musical careers. It's not that we give up music at the expense of our relationship, but our marriage is our number one priority. So when my wife has a performance scheduled abroad, I look into whether I can also give a concert in the same place or at least the same country during that time so that we can travel together. Usually it's possible, and then our little girl travels with us. We have hired an absolute gem of a governess who takes care of her when we are both working, and it works perfectly for everyone."

"That's fantastic to hear, Max. By the way, I was very emotional when I received your birth announcement. Did you name her after me?"

Max smiles and replies, "I think it's a very beautiful and meaningful name."

Appendix:
A Discussion of Bullying

The author conducted interviews with child psychologists, organizations, parents, teachers, victims, and bullies. This is a representation of what emerged from that research.

Although bullying, humiliation, and assault have been around for a long time, it does not mean that we should accept it.

There is no valid reason to physically attack, punch, kick, and humiliate one another. Bullying is even prohibited by law. There are international rights that protect every child, ensuring they can grow up safely.

If you are being bullied, there is one thing you need to know: *it is not your fault.*

What Bullying Is

The basis of bullying is fear: instilling fear and being afraid. Bullying at school is a group activity. It is about exerting power over others. It starts with teasing, which is often repeated. It can happen every day or once a week. It can escalate into sadism. If the victim does not react, the bully does not know how far they can go, so they continue.

Bullying always involves three elements:
- It occurs repeatedly against the same person.
- It involves inequality (in power, strength, or social status).
- It is intentional.

There are different forms of bullying.

Verbal Bullying
- Teasing, using derogatory names, insulting, taunting, imitating, ridiculing, or mocking
- Commenting on clothing or appearance (especially by girls)
- Threatening, coercing, blackmailing, or intimidating

Physical Bullying
- Physical violence through fighting, kicking, hitting, and spitting (especially among boys), or pinching (more common among girls).

Material Bullying
- Breaking, taking away, or hiding belongings.

Relational Bullying
- Isolating a person from the group, especially through gossiping or spreading rumors about someone. Looking at someone with a disdainful gaze.

Digital Bullying
- Also known as *cyberbullying* or online *bullying*. Harassing someone through social media by spreading compromising photos, videos, or rumors.

Sexual Bullying
- Verbal, nonverbal, or physical behavior with a sexual connotation, often targeting girls. From early exposure to pornography (sometimes as young as seven or eight years old), boys may come to believe that the sexual world depicted there is reality. They imitate what they see and think a woman is an object of desire to be treated as one pleases.

How Does Bullying Originate?

It can start as early as four or five years old, although bullying at that age is different from when one is older. Often young children don't understand that they are being bullied. It's less calculated and more about determining who is the strongest.

During this period, a child learns to deal with their emotions. We need to get to know and understand our emotions, such as fear, anger, and frustration when faced with danger. "I react, you react" helps establish boundaries. If you can't express emotions, you become like a robot.

Being part of a group helps in developing emotions. Without negative emotions, you won't be able to react. If a child hasn't learned this at home because their parents don't communicate much with them, they won't be able to express themselves verbally. In essence, they are not connected with themselves, causing disharmony.

Bullying becomes more conscious, more perverse, and meaner during adolescence.

With girls, you see bullying happening very subtly through looks, words, and attitudes. The bully looks for something to unsettle the other person, sometimes out of revenge. Often the girls were friends before, but one may have said something that didn't sit well with the other, or one gets a boyfriend and the other becomes jealous.

Bullying continues because the victim doesn't establish their boundaries.

Teenagers are especially vulnerable during puberty because of hormonal changes. During this period, they break away from their parents and seek connection with a new group—one that provides them with stability, even if they disagree with its rules. Adolescents may accept humiliation in order to belong (this is often observed with girls). Alternatively, they may fear expressing their boundaries within the group as a result of shame and fear of rejection.

Bullying can also occur when parents have little time for the teenager or fail to listen to them. The teenager then seeks connection with their own group, for example at school.

Why in a Group?

It is a fundamental human need to be part of a group. We need it to feel safe and protected; it's an innate feeling. We cannot survive alone, so rejection is very painful. We look up to leaders. We see them as heroes and seek to be recognized like them. (This can still be observed even in higher education.) We search for role models and gravitate towards the strongest individuals in the group. There are different roles within a group: the leader and the followers.

There are many different groups within a classroom. Within each one, there are people who are dominant and people who are dominated. Someone who is dominant wants to be in charge.

Followers lack self-confidence. They are fascinated by the power of their leader. If you are close to a bully within a group, you know that you won't be bullied yourself. The bully's followers feel safe. If children were given the choice between being bullied or being the bully, they would choose to be the bully.

Each group has its own code, and an outsider joining the group can disrupt the balance. You cannot join a group if you are different. Everyone has their place.

Why doesn't the group accept you when you're different?

When someone new joins a group, they bring new energy to the group. Even a child who was not previously bullied can become a victim in such a situation. The group does not accept differences. It's like a herd of animals. Someone who is different constitutes a threat to the group. Humans want control and certainty, so being different is not accepted. The leader is afraid that the newcomer could become stronger, so they bully them out of fear of being bullied themselves.

Bullying does not involve the bully and the victim alone; others are involved. Bullying is a group process with different roles. There are six roles:

1. **The victim.** The one being bullied.
2. **The bully.** The one who initiates the bullying.
3. **The assistant.** The one who doesn't start the bullying themselves but joins in once someone else has started. The assistant helps the bully.
4. **The reinforcer.** The one who doesn't bully directly but laughs at the bully or encourages them. The reinforcer makes the bully feel that bullying is fun or funny.
5. **The defender.** The one who helps the victim, for example, by telling the bully to stop or by reporting the bullying to the teacher.
6. **The bystander.** The one who usually knows that bullying is happening but does not get involved. This can make the victim feel that the bystander doesn't mind the bullying. Additionally, the bully may feel that their behavior is acceptable.

Who Are the Victims?

Victims are typically different from the other children, for example, taller, shorter, fatter, or thinner. They may feel vulnerable. They can have a negative self-image and do not believe in themselves. Deep down, they are anxious, and the bully exacerbates this fear. Bullying happens to children who also live in a fantasy world, are highly gifted, or distant. In the case of a boy, it could be that he has an aggressive father who abuses his mother. The child feels guilty because he cannot protect his mother and doubts himself.

The Bully

A bully is often someone who is not confident in themselves but wants to feel stronger than someone else, often to hide their own insecurities or to avoid being bullied themselves. When other group members laugh at what they do, they feel more powerful, and the game continues. Unknowingly, they end up in a position of power without being aware of the harm they inflict on the victim.

It's the power of the strongest. The bully and the victim are drawn to each other. It could be that the victim initially admires someone in the class who is dominant. The bully senses that the other person has little self-confidence and gradually takes control of them.

The bully may mimic behavior from home because one of their parents is very dominant or violent. Or they themselves are teased, neglected, ignored, or scorned by their parents. They lack sufficient support at home and seek a position of power outside. But being a bully doesn't have to be a lifelong role.

What characterizes bullies?
- They fight against their own fear or live in an artificial world.
- They are narcissistic, lack self-confidence, or have a personality disorder.
- They insult others to gain more appreciation for themselves.
- They want control or power over someone else.
- They are manipulative, with strong personalities.
- They often derive pleasure from causing pain or humiliation to others (sadism). A bully needs excitement and enjoys playing cat-and-mouse games.

The Victim
- At first, the victim often doesn't realize they are being bullied.
- Losing self-confidence is a consequence of bullying.
- The victim may be afraid to talk to their parents out of fear of criticism, not being believed, or disappointing the parents.
- The victim may not receive enough support at home.
- They may think it's normal to be humiliated.
- They may be angry at themselves, asking, "Why do I allow this?"
- They may have little or no confidence in themselves.

- They may think they are bad.
- They may believe they can't defend themselves.
- They may be shy and anxious.
- They can be too serious, not understanding jokes.
- They may ask themselves, "What do others think of me?"
- They may think it's their fault that they are called names.
- They want the pain of bullying to stop.
- They often want to be left alone.
- They may want to find a solution on their own.
- They often have difficulty expressing themselves.
- They can be withdrawn.
- They may develop different strategies to avoid the bully.
- They may think, "I can't make friends."

Symptoms of Being Bullied
- Silence
- Moodiness
- Being defiant or rebellious
- Conflicts at home or school
- Scratches and bruises
- Torn clothing
- A backpack or schoolbag that suddenly goes missing
- Loss of interest in learning; sudden low grades at school
- Trouble concentrating
- Sleep problems
- Bedwetting

- Stomachaches before going to school
- Avoiding school
- Lack of interest in playing
- Having no friends or very few
- Isolating themselves
- Headaches
- Significant weight gain
- Significant weight loss; loss of appetite
- Suicide or suicide attempts

Solutions

If you think you are a victim of bullying, ask yourself the following questions:

- Why does the other person have power while I don't?
- Why didn't I defend myself? (It is every person's duty to defend themselves when in danger.)
- Whom have I discussed this with? Have I asked for help?
- Have I informed a teacher, school counselor, or trusted adult?
- Has the school taken action to protect me? If not, what steps can I take with the help of my parents or a trusted adult?
- Do I feel safe in this school? If not, what are my options—and who can help me explore them?

Actions to Take
- Work on your self-image and self-confidence.
- Step out of the victim role. You *were* a victim, but *you are not* a victim. Stepping out of the victim role gives a different perspective.
- Know yourself. What are your strengths? What do you love?
- Learn to unconditionally love yourself; be your own best friend.
- When experiencing fear, return to important values such as safety, respect, privacy, freedom of speech, gratitude, friendship, self-control, and enjoyment.
- Learn to recognize your emotions. How does it feel to be angry, upset, or happy? How do you handle them? Also, learn how to avoid defaulting to anger.
- Live in the present moment—not in the past or in the future.
- Live from within. Don't depend on what happens in the outside world, or you will be controlled by it.
- Learn to defend yourself.
- Engage in physical activity; participate in sports.
- Practice certain skills. Being good at something boosts your self-confidence and makes you feel worthy.
- Choose an artistic hobby, such as painting or theater. Find a creative outlet that you enjoy.
- Achieve successes.

- Spend time with those who share your interests.
- Learn to say no.
- Learn to communicate.
- Know your boundaries. Define your personal space. What is your limit? When is someone crossing it?
- Seek help. Talk to a trusted person, whether it's parents or friends.
- To stop bullying, it needs to be exposed. If no one sees it, no one can help.
- How can you feel safe at school?

Tips for Victims

- Never respond to the bully with similar aggression.
- Children who act like clowns are not bullied, even though they are different.
- Find a funny response. For example, if a bully says, "You're ugly, and you stink," look the bully directly in the eyes in a natural but fearless manner and respond, "Oh, that's my natural perfume." Result: the bully loses because what he says no longer affects you, especially if other group members laugh at your response. The bully will leave you alone in the future.
- Practice your responses at home with a sibling or a good friend so that you appear confident when responding to the bully.

Tips for Parents
- Say "I love you" and show your love; it's never too late.
- Pay attention to your language. Avoid negative comments about yourself, such as "Oh, I'm so stupid!" or "What a fool I am!"
- Don't be too protective of your child. Don't perform extremely simple tasks for them, because that shows you have little or no confidence in them.
- Take the time to listen to your child's needs; let them talk and listen.
- Give your child the chance to express their feelings.
- Be present for your child.
- Be alert. Observe sudden changes in behavior and intervene in time. Observe their eating, sleeping, and playing habits. If a child is not playing, something is wrong; it's not normal.
- Don't be too strict.
- Don't treat your child like a baby.
- Teach your child to win and lose by playing board games. Don't let them win all the time.

Suggestions for Schools
- Teach children from a young age how to live with each other, establish relationships, and interact with one another.
- Allow children the opportunity to express their fears.

- Give children occasions to play board games.
- Observe students who are different. Keep an eye on whether they are being bullied.
- Allow children to express themselves verbally and through drawing.
- Encourage working in small groups and group discussions. Teach respectful communication.
- Create opportunities in role-playing games, in which children learn to put themselves in others' shoes.
- Teach children what to say in tense or hostile situations.
- On the playground, teach children how to play with each other, respect each other, and follow rules.
- Create tasks and responsibilities that foster self-respect.
- Teach empathy.
- Focus on equality and respect.
- Reduce the current emphasis on competition, whereby only the winner counts.
- Give more attention to teaching skills.

General Information

- Children want to be loved and recognized. They don't want to be excluded.
- Raising a child in a balanced way requires a mother for developing self-confidence and a father for developing awareness. These roles can also be filled by, for example, an uncle or aunt, a sports coach, or teacher.

- Children succeed and thrive when they feel valued, supported, and uplifted. They need others who encourage them. Later in life, it could be a colleague or a partner.
- Teach children to defend themselves with nonaggressive words.
- Attitude is also important, as well as self-confidence, which can be gained through activities like judo or other sports. Girls benefit greatly from dancing and sports, especially fencing, which helps them command respect and establish boundaries.
- Perfect harmony doesn't exist in a group; there are always differences, as well as leader and followers.
- Nowadays a lot of violence, blackmail, and humiliation is shown on television almost around the clock. Reduce exposure to violent or exploitative television programs.
- Parents should beware of the messages they send when discussing their own lives, such as talking about how someone has belittled a colleague or achieved a promotion at the expense of another person. Notice also the effects of talking about work pressure and complaints about the exploitative behavior of bosses or supervisors. It is very confusing for a child to hear about abusive or disrespectful behavior among adults.
- Many children are frustrated.
- Bullying has existed for a long time, but thanks to a number of national and international laws and conventions, it is no longer permitted.

Current Social Problems

Because of social media, teenagers don't take the time to build friendships in real life. Their conversations are frequently empty, even superficial, and they may not even know basic things about one another. They frequently show lack of mutual respect and a neglect of boundaries.

Nowadays, language is much more violent than before. Children feel compelled to use it in order to fit in with the group. They often tend to see themselves externally rather than from within. Teens are frequently lonely, vulnerable, and suspicious.

Bullying can have lasting effects in adult life, especially if it is not recognized or acknowledged during the school years. A person who has been bullied may experience anxiety and stress, producing posttraumatic symptoms.

Adults who have been bullied struggle with interacting with others. They may cling to their victim role and often belittle themselves. They may lack belief in themselves and have difficulty saying no and standing up for themselves. They may prefer to remain silent and can attract dominant partners, friends, colleagues, or superiors. They may become depressed and prone to burnout. Often it comes out only in later stages of therapy that they were bullied in school.

Acknowledgments

I would like to express my gratitude to:

Clients and friends who encouraged me to write this book. In particular, I would like to mention Sandrine Ngoma, Vincent Rubinno, and Jonathan Horton.

José van Winden, who helped me edit the very first version of this manuscript with care and insight. It was a pleasure to work with her in those early stages.

The many psychologists who generously gave their time to help bring this book to life.

Victims, parents of victims, and bullies who allowed me to interview them.

I am also grateful and indebted to the countless mentors who have shared their wisdom and helped me become the woman I am today. I would like to mention a few of them here. Forgive me if your name is not mentioned; my gratitude is no less:

Anthony Robbins; Louise Hay; Dr. Wayne Dyer; Bob Proctor; Brian Proctor and Cory Kelly Proctor; Esther Hicks and Abraham; Gloria and Kenneth Wapnick; Marianne Williamson; Julia Hastings; Willem de Ridder; Peggy McColl; T. Harv

Eker; Phil Laut; Yohann Duclos; Shirzad Chamine; and Bill Carmody.

I would also like to thank my agent, **Dan Strutzel**, for believing in me and in this book, and for the inspiring and smooth collaboration.

My heartfelt thanks go as well to **G&D Media** and their wonderful creative team for their support and dedication. Thanks to you, this book could find its way into the world.

And to you, dear reader:

Thank you for choosing this book and giving it your time and attention. This is not just a book to read; it's a book to apply. I hope it has offered you insights, encouragement, and practical tools to help you reconnect with your inner strength. Remember: no matter where you come from or what you've been through, transformation is always possible.

You are not alone.

You matter.

You are stronger than you think.

Thank you for letting me be part of your story.

Resources

Books

Stella Adler, *The Art of Acting*
James Allen, *As a Man Thinketh*
Rhonda Byrne, *The Secret*; *The Magic*
Dale Carnegie, *How to Win Friends and Influence People*
Gary Chapman, *Teen's Guide to the Five Love Languages: How to Understand Yourself and Improve All Your Relationships*
Shirzad Charmine, *Positive Intelligence*
Paulo Coelho, *The Alchemist*
A Course in Miracles
Joe Dispenza, *Becoming Supernatural*
Julia Hastings, *Visualize Your Desires*; *You Are Worth Gold*; *The Daydream Diet*
Louise Hay, *You Can Heal Your Life*; *I Love My Body*; *Thoughts of Inner Wisdom*; *Living in the Now*; *Using Your Inner Power*; and *Healing Meditation*
Esther and Jerry Hicks, *Ask and It Is Given*; *Getting into the Vortex*; and *The Law of Attraction*

Napoleon Hill, *Think and Grow Rich*

Raymond Holliwell, *Working with the Laws*

Gerald G. Jampolsky and Diane V. Cirincione, *Love Is the Answer*

Leil Lowndes, *How to Talk to Anyone: 92 Little Tricks for Big Success in Relationships*

Maxwell Maltz, *The New Psycho-Cybernetics*

Joseph Murphy, *The Power of Your Subconscious Mind*

Neville, *The Essential Collection*

Norman Vincent Peale, *The Power of Enthusiasm*

Bob Proctor, *You Were Born Rich*

Anthony Robbins, *Awaken the Giant Within*

Eckhart Tolle, *The Power of Now*

Marianne Williamson, *A Return to Love*

Counseling

If you're struggling with bullying or emotional pain, please don't keep it to yourself. Asking for help is not a weakness: it's a sign of strength.

There are people who care, and organizations that are available for you, day or night.

In the United States:
- The Trevor Project (for LGBTQ+ youth): thetrevorproject.org. Call 1-866-488-7386. Available 24/7.
- Crisis Text Line (also supports bullying-related crises): crisistextline.org. Text HELLO to 741741. Available 24/7

- PACER's National Bullying Prevention Center: pacer.org/bullying. Email: bullying411@pacer.org. Personal support and guidance via email and online resources.

In the United Kingdom:
- Childline (for children and teens up to nineteen): childline.org.uk. Call 0800 1111. Free, confidential, available 24/7.
- Family Lives/Bullying UK (for children and parents): bullying.co.uk. Call 0808 800 2222.

You are not alone.
There is hope. There is help.
And you are worth it.

About the Author

Ria Berkhout is a teacher, mentor, and author who supports teenagers in overcoming the emotional wounds caused by bullying. Her work focuses on helping teens rebuild their self-confidence, feel safe again, and restore joy and a deep sense of self-worth.

For more than thirty years, Ria has studied the power of thoughts, self-image psychology, emotional resilience, and universal laws such as the law of attraction. Her work is grounded, heart-centered, and rooted in everything she once longed to receive as a teenager herself.

She now lives in the French countryside, where she writes, teaches, and continues to inspire others through her deep passion for personal growth and emotional freedom.

Ria has designed a unique and transformational program for teens and parents based on decades of personal experience, intensive study, and interviews with victims, parents, psychologists, teachers, and even bullies. The program offers practical guidance for emotional healing, clear communication, and reclaiming inner strength—for both teens and the adults who support them. To learn more about Ria and her course, visit www.ria-berkhout.com.